D0039472

HOW TO REMEMBER JOKES

AND 101 DROP-DEAD JOKES TO GET YOU STARTED

HOW TO REMEMBER JOKES

AND 101 DROP-DEAD JOKES TO GET YOU STARTED

BY PHILIP VAN MUNCHING

ILLUSTRATIONS BY
ELWOOD H. SMITH

WORKMAN PUBLISHING · NEW YORK

Text Copyright © 1997 by Philip Van Munching

Illustrations Copyright © 1997 by Elwood H. Smith

All rights reserved. No portion of this book may be reproduced—
mechanically, electronically, or by any other means, including
photocopying—without written permission of the publisher.
Published simultaneously in Canada by Thomas Allen & Son Limited.

Van Munching, Philip.

How to remember jokes: an idiot-proof system for the bashful, the forgetful, the tongue-tied
& the humor impaired, and 101 drop-dead jokes to get you started/by Philip Van Munching:
illustrations by Elwood H. Smith.

p. cm.

ISBN 0-7611-0734-7

1. American wit and humor. 2. Mnemonics. I. Title.

PN6162.V28 1997

808.7—dc21

97-35577

CIP

Cover and book design by Lisa Hollander

Workman Publishing

708 Broadway

New York, NY 10003-9555

First printing October 1997

Manufactured in the United States of America

10 9 8 7 6 5 4 3 2 1

For J.R. Pratt, Bill Holding,
Len Schlachter,
and Peter Workman...

...this book is their fault.

With my thanks to
Sally Kovalchick,
John Meils, Alden Ludlow,
and the guy at
Robin Dodge's dinner
party who told
"François  François"

It's really rather odd that you have a hard time recalling jokes. When you stop to think about it, a joke is nothing more than a story with a payoff—which is like the content of most everyday conversation. When your friend tells you something embarrassing that his or her spouse did, you have no trouble repeating the story to *your* spouse who's on the verge of doing the same dopey thing three days later. Your boss bores you silly with his vacation exploits, but you can remember every dull detail when you laughingly recount them to your coworker over lunch. Your memory for stories, it seems, is just fine.

So why can't you remember jokes? The simple answer is this: You don't make an effort to commit them to memory. The word *effort* probably scared off half the people who were thumbing through this book in favor of the new Grisham novel. Let them go. The effort involved in remembering jokes is minimal, and once made, becomes completely natural. But before you dive in, a quick and painless stroll through how memory works will give you the necessary background to make remembering jokes a snap.

Think Cue, Think Cue Very Much

AND THE DUCK SAID.... NO, WAIT... THE COW....THE... ... WAIT...

Professor Daniel L. Schacter solves one of life's great mysteries in his book *Searching for Memory*: the trouble with remembering phone numbers. Why is it that once you've used the phone book or dialed information to get a number, you have to repeat it to yourself like mad until you've punched it into the phone? According to Schacter, it's because you approach the act of remembering different types of information in different ways. In the case of a phone number, you keep it by using a more superficial part of memory called the phonological loop (no pun intended). You do this because—in most cases—your need for this information won't last more than several seconds.

Facts you have some reason to retain, you thrust deeper into your memory through a process known as *encoding*, which involves building associations between the new information and older information already residing in your brain. You already know the inherent value of encoding—it's why you use your mother's birthday as the secret code for your bank card, or the batting average of your favorite ballplayer as the combination to your briefcase lock. Those numbers carry more meaning for you than randomly selected three- or four-digit numbers.

Encoding processes, which are ways of cementing pieces of information into memory, are at the center of any number of "improve your memory" books and audiotapes, including several by the undisputed king of memory systems, Harry Lorayne. At the center of Lorayne's teachings is something called the "link system," which involves mentally connecting items in exaggerated ways to create humorous or outlandish mental images using the things that need to be remembered. For example, let's say you have some errands to run, and on those errands you need to buy sheets for the bed, a new hammer, and a bag of potato chips. Before you head out the door, you might take a moment to visualize a giant hammer sleeping in a bed, with a new sheet pulled up the length of the grip. Then you might visualize that giant hammer smashing a bag of chips. As long as you can remember the first thing, sheets, you will have embedded the other two through these outrageous mental images.

This method works if you have lists of things to remember. It doesn't work so well if you're trying to remember a joke or a story, although it holds an important piece of the memory puzzle: the cue. Think of cues, or reminders, as the keys that unlock memories. You see the face of an old friend from school, and you suddenly remember something that happened in junior high. A colleague mentions an Italian restaurant she'd like to go to and you're instantly reminded of the pasta sauce you wanted to make. The old "tie-a-ribbon-around-your-finger" trick is nothing more than a mental cue taken to an extreme.

You remember everyday stories because they have so many cues built into them. For example, an old friend tells you a story about how his four-year-old daughter asked him what a "watergate" was and how a gate could ever hold water. Obviously, the child had heard the word on a news program and misunderstood. (This example is intentionally not that funny; if it were a riot, you could argue that it's easy to remember because you busted your gut laughing.) Here are the cues that might help you recall the story: the mention of your friend or of old friends in general; the mention of children, or more specifically that "children say the darndest things"; the mention of that child in particular; or the mention of Watergate. Any of these things could *cue* your memory to the content of that story.

One simple cue by itself rarely stirs the memory of an entire joke. Even when someone tells a lawyer joke, and you *recall* that you heard another good lawyer joke, it's still not enough to remind you what the darn joke was. This is why you're going to learn to identify

BILL OF GOODS

A joke is nothing more than a story with a payoff at the end. It has a setup, in which you describe the scene and the characters ("A duck walks into a pharmacy . . ."). It has action or dialogue (". . . and asks the pharmacist for a Chap Stick. The pharmacist asks if the duck is paying cash."). It concludes with a payoff, or punchline ("'No,' says the duck, 'just put it on my bill.'")

numbers of cues within each joke you read on these pages—or any joke you hear.

What sets jokes apart from true stories is that you tend to listen to jokes with more of an emphasis on the punchline than on the buildup. We don't count on true stories to have much of an ending—we see them as streams of information in which importance is almost equally weighted from the setup to the payoff. To learn to remember jokes, you have to retrain your brain to absorb them as if they were true stories, and cues are a big help in doing so.

The Quest for Cues

Aside from the actual content of jokes, cues can come from the type and **category** of a joke you've just heard. Jokes tend to be organized in three ways: the straight story, the repeated-action story with an unexpected result (see "François François" on pages 9–10), and the play on words (the punchlines of these jokes are popular titles or phrases slightly altered to comic effect, like "Rudolph the Red knows rain, dear."). Except for jokes that feature a play on words, the *type* of joke isn't usually enough to cue the memory of another joke.

Categories are a lot more useful. Classic jokes come in endless variations, but most tend to fall within the eleven categories listed here. The most popular categories, in no particular order, are:

- Barroom jokes ("A guy walks into a bar . . .")

- Lawyer jokes

- Bawdy jokes (As Tom Lehrer once sang, "Filth, I'm glad to say, is in the mind of the beholder.")

- Topical jokes ("Jimmy Carter, Richard Nixon, and Ted Kennedy are on a boat . . .")

- Classroom jokes (Most of these feature the foul-mouthed "Little Eddie.")

- Golf jokes

- Genie jokes (in which someone is granted three wishes)

- Religion jokes (most notably God jokes and Pope jokes)

- Pearly Gates jokes (The entrance to heaven may be second only to the barroom as the most popular setting for humor.)

- Groaners (almost exclusively "play on words" jokes, which tend to make you groan at their sheer corniness rather than laugh)

- General (everything that doesn't fit neatly into one of the first ten categories)

Each category provides a cue to get you thinking about a type of joke. How many times have you heard a Pearly Gates joke, for example, and know that you have recently heard another great Pearly Gates but can't remember what it was? The trick is to build a few other simple cues into specific jokes so that the category cue is enough to start a mental chain reaction.

...AND HOW ABOUT THIS ONE...

When trying to recall a true story, your memory is aided by whatever previously absorbed knowledge you have of the story's participants. When you hear that something happened to someone you know, you can't help but mentally picture his or her face. In jokes, this doesn't happen because the characters don't exist; they're created to serve the plot.

If you want to make jokes memorable, make the characters more real—give them a face and a voice in your imagination. In other words, **cast the parts,** just as you imagine what the protagonist looks like when you read a novel. The act of mentally casting jokes provides the brain with as many cues as there are parts to cast, thus further solidifying them in your memory.

In addition to using real characters as a memory device, it helps to imagine a place you know as a joke setting, or **location.** If you hear a joke about a guy who walks into a bar, make it a bar you know. If you hear a joke about students in a classroom, remember a classroom you were in or one you saw on television. The locations don't have to be drawn from memory; they just have to be drawn, period. The act of imagining what a setting would look like—the waiting area outside the Pearly Gates, for an oft-used example—helps solidify that setting in your brain.

CASTING CALL

My father-in-law and I spent considerable time casting our fantasy movie version of Nelson DeMille's hilarious novel *The Gold Coast*—William Hurt, Jessica Lange, and Chazz Palminteri made our final cut— and I found that my memory of the book's plot solidified once I could picture those actors in it. That said, I almost never use actors when I mentally cast jokes. I use real people I have some chance of running into or being reminded of, like my favorite bartender or lawyer.

Once you've got mental pictures of the people and places in the jokes you hear, it isn't a stretch to **picture the action** within a given joke, relating it to real-life experience whenever possible. There must be three or four jokes in this book that start with a golfer slicing his shot into the woods. Anyone who's ever tried to hit a golf ball has done this, so it shouldn't be hard for a golfer of any skill level to hear or read one of these jokes and recall instantly the frustration of a really bad slice. Cheer up, duffers; that bad slice happens to be a good memory cue.

No single one of these tricks is very convincing as a memory aid, but when used together, these memory triggers are nearly infallible. From now on, you'll have at least four distinctive mental cues that you can easily build into every joke you hear: categorization (what kind of joke is it?), casting (who's in it?), location (where does it take place?), and action (what happens?). Once you practice using these elements as memory cues, you'll see how little effort it takes to remember jokes. Especially if you reinforce them by using a time-tested memory trick—repetition.

Repeat After Me

The main reason people forget jokes is that they don't repeat them quickly enough. If asked immediately after hearing a joke to repeat it, most people are perfectly capable of doing so. It's that lag time between last Thursday's dinner party and next Tuesday's coffee break that seems to kill the ability to remember.

So don't wait so long. If fact, don't wait at all. If you take one thing away from this book, let it be this: *If you want to remember a joke, tell it to someone as quickly as you can after hearing it.* At a party, find someone who wasn't within earshot when the joke was told to you, and tell it to them. If you hear a joke at work, phone someone you know who appreciates jokes and repeat it to them. (Don't get caught by your boss—getting fired in the middle of telling a joke absolutely destroys your ability to tell it well.) You'll find that mental cues are cemented a little more with each retelling.

Some years ago, as a dull stretch threatened to end an otherwise reasonably interesting dinner party, a friend of the hostess uncorked the following classic. In the—I kid you not—two full minutes of laughter that followed the punchline, there were nearly three deaths, a slight (though unverified) pants-wetting, and two spilled glasses of wine. The party was saved (but the tablecloth didn't make it). And this particular joke is an excellent example of the final piece of the memory puzzle, which involves titling jokes in such a way that not only reinforces them in your mind, but doesn't give away the punchline.

A Classic Dinner Party Joke

Right at the end of World War II, a young American woman wanders into a bar in Paris, where she sees a handsome young Frenchman. They make some eye contact, and soon he comes up to her and says, "I am François François, ze great French aviator, and I want to make love to you."

"Yes," she says. "Take me to your apartment."

Once there, François François undresses her, and as they start to make love, he pulls out a stick of butter and rubs it on her chest.

"François François, what are you doing?" she asks.

He says, "I am François François, ze great French aviator, and when I make love to a woman, I like to lick butter from her breasts." Clearly enjoying this, she lets him continue.

He moves his attention farther down her body, and pulls out a bottle of chocolate syrup, which he pours on her navel.

"François François, what are you doing?" she asks.

He says, "I am François François, ze great French aviator, and when I make love to a woman, I like to lick chocolate from her belly button." Writhing in pleasure, she lets him continue.

Moving farther down, he pulls out a bottle of olive oil, which he spreads on her abdomen.

"François François, what are you doing?" she asks.

He says, "I am François François, ze great French aviator, and when I make love to a woman I like to lick extra virgin olive oil from just above her nether region." She's almost unable to bear all of the pleasure.

When he's done with the olive oil, François François pulls out a bottle of brandy, which he pours on her "nether region." Then he pulls out a match, lights it, and throws it onto the brandy as she screams, "FRANÇOIS FRANÇOIS, WHAT ARE YOU DOING?"

And he says, "I am François François, ze great French aviator, and when I go down, I go down in flames!"

Tame It with a Title

Titles are what we use to identify things—television programs, books, films, songs. Instead of asking someone if they saw the movie about the great white shark that terrorizes a New England resort community, you ask them if they saw *Jaws*. Titles make it easier to differentiate among a number of similar things, as well. If you ask a friend whether they watch the TV show about young roommates, you could be talking about half the programs in prime time these days. If you say *Friends*, they know what you mean.

But titles aren't only for identification; in most cases, they're used to represent content, as well. The appellation *Jaws*, once you know anything about the film plot, is evocative enough to be easily remembered through basic association: It's about a shark that eats people. Similarly, *Raging Bull* is about a great fighter who can't control his temper. Although they don't always provide a clear indication (can you tell me what the John Hughes movie *Some Kind of Wonderful* is about?), titles can help you remember the content of jokes.

Titling becomes particularly useful when it comes to remembering jokes if you want to avoid the most common mistake joke tellers make: the ruinous over-description. By way of illustration, a true story:

A few years ago, a woman finds a huge bug in her kitchen. Terrified, she nabs the bug, runs it into the bathroom, and flushes it down the toilet. Still scared, she empties a can of bug spray into the bowl for good measure. Ten minutes later, her husband comes home. He goes right for the john, and while he's in there he smokes a cigarette. He tosses the last of the cigarette into the bowl *while* he's on it, and the chemicals from the bug spray burst into flame, burning him in some very sensitive places. Now the paramedics come. They load him up on a stretcher, which they have to carry down a flight of stairs because the apartment is on the second floor and there isn't an elevator. While they're on the stairs, the woman finishes telling them how her husband got the burns. They start laughing so hard, they lose their balance and drop him down the stairs.

Notice, this is not a joke. There's no punchline, only a short series of absurd events. If you wanted to tell someone this story, would you start by saying, "Hey, did you hear about the guy who got blown up on the toilet and dropped down the stairs by medics?

Many people, when about to tell a joke, ask something like "Hey, did you hear the one about the three stupid hunters who are trying to figure out what kind of tracks they've found?" Usually, it's done to avoid the embarrassment of launching into a joke only to have someone say "heard it" or, even worse, have someone else finish it. By applying the strategy of titling, you can concisely represent the joke you're about to tell *without* giving away all the good stuff. And it's another great way to remember the content. It's a three-step process: Pick out what's important in a joke, boil down those elements into the least amount of words or phrases possible, and arrange those words or phrases into a title.

By using the basic method of association—using each important item to remember related details—a joke as long as "François François" becomes manageable. The important things in that joke are François's habit of giving his name and occupation (because it's absurd, and doing his accent makes the joke fun to tell), the fact that he narrates his own lovemaking in such detail, and the punchline. What's *not* important are the details of his lovemaking, which make up the bulk of the joke. It doesn't matter if you tell the joke with whipped cream, chocolate, or syrup. Yet that's precisely the area where most people get hung up. They want to get it exactly right, then they sputter over each part where François tells his lover what he likes to do. There's nothing worse than having someone stop in the middle of a joke to try to remember a detail.

When we break down the joke to its basic elements, we end up with the protagonist's name (François François, ze great French aviator); what he does ("When I make love to a woman, I like to lick [blank] from her [blank]"); and the punchline ("When I go down, I go

WHAT'S IN A NAME?

The wrong joke title can be the kiss of death. For example, first time novelist John Gilstrap got nowhere trying to sell a suspense thriller he'd titled *Nathan!* Publishers uniformly rejected his manuscript until someone got the bright idea of dropping the silly exclamation point and renaming the book *Nathan's Run.* Suddenly, the book (and film rights) sold for a small fortune, and Gilstrap found himself profiled in *People.*

Actor Hugh Grant wasn't so lucky. His follow-up to the hugely successful *Four Weddings and a Funeral* was the horribly over-named *The Englishman Who Went Up a Hill But Came Down a Mountain.* This was a perfectly genial comedy, but it drew about as many patrons as it had words in the title.

down in flames!"). Each point should be considered when picking a title.

And if you can apply some simple associations, there's not much to memorize. The first point gives you François's name and occupation (and though not overtly stated, you can guess his nationality, the time setting, and general locale). The second point gives you the guts of the joke—his sexual technique through a series of actions moving down the woman's body. The third point, of course, is the payoff.

In the case of this joke, most people find it unnecessary to force themselves to remember even François's occupation, because once you've said the phrase "I am François François, ze great French aviator" a few times (it's said five times just by telling the joke *once*), it gets ingrained. The man's name becomes enough to remember occupation, nationality, and setting. So, the first titling point has been whittled down to "François François." The second point, the action of the joke, isn't that he's making love to a woman, it's *how* he's doing it. The "how" is important, because it implies the step-by-step process that gives the joke its story. The third point, or the punchline, is crucial because the more you look at it or repeat it, the quicker you're going to memorize it. And you should memorize it, because putting it in the title would sort of defeat the purpose.

You're left with "How François François Makes Love." And not only will that title help you associatively remember the joke, it will safely bear the prefix "Did you hear the one about . . ."

The great thing about titling is that it's not static. Once you've told a joke like "How François François Makes Love" a few times, you'll find your title can be shortened. (My wife loves the joke—or at least she's indulgent enough of me to swear that she does—and she's heard me tell it so many times that it's become "François" to her.) There's a title for each of the remaining 101 jokes in this collection. Test them out, kick the tires. If you don't find them useful, use this strategy to come up with one of your own.

A Road Map to Remembering

In addition to a title, each joke that follows is outfitted with potential memory cues listed by icon. At the end of each joke, the category, the mental casting and location possibilities, and any recognizable action (like slicing a golf shot) are given. Here's how the list of memory cues for "How François François Makes Love" would look:

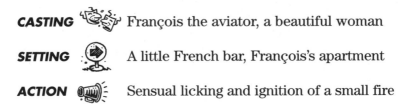

• B A W D Y •

CASTING — François the aviator, a beautiful woman

SETTING — A little French bar, François's apartment

ACTION — Sensual licking and ignition of a small fire

Remember, the notes that follow each joke are meant to give you ideas for creating cues that will work for *you*. The best aid to remembering any of these jokes, of course, is repetition, so tell the ones you like best to your friends, family, or any warm body you can find with a sense of humor. Read them aloud if you think that will work for you. Anything that gets them filtered through your brain and past your lips will help you remember them.

Oh, and have you heard the one about . . .

101 CLASSIC JOKES TO TRAIN YOUR BRAIN

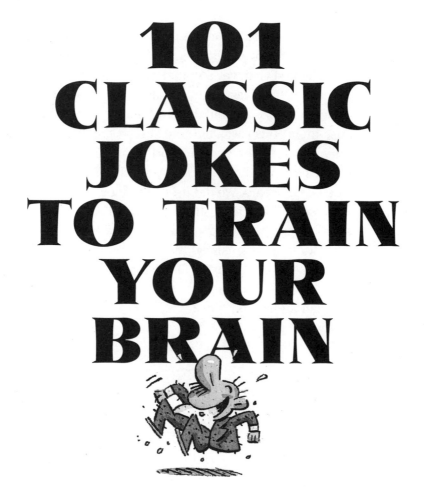

The Old Man's Confession

An old man steps into a confessional and says, "Father, I've been married for over 50 years, and I've always been faithful to my wife. I've never so much as *looked* at another woman in all that time—until last night. While my wife was out playing bridge, my neighbor's 18-year-old daughter came over to borrow a flashlight because their power was out and she was alone. 'Stay here, I've got electricity,' I said to her, and she said, 'You sure do,' and started taking my clothes off. We did it, Father. We did it more times than I've done it in the last 30 years. We did it on the floor, on the table, on the bed, in the shower . . . and then she went home."

"Well," says the priest, "you've tried to be a good husband, and I think the Lord knows that you resisted temptation for half a century, and He appreciates it. So, if you say 10 Our Fathers and 10 Hail Marys and . . ."

"Father," the man interrupts, "I'm Jewish, not Catholic."

"Well then, why are you telling me all of this?" the priest asks.

"Telling you? I'm telling everyone!"

• B A W D Y / R E L I G I O N •

 An old man, a priest

 A confessional

 A priest hears an adulterous confession.

Two Men Compare Death Stories

Two men waiting at the Pearly Gates strike up a conversation.

"How'd you die?" the first man asks the second.

"I froze to death," says the second.

"That's awful," says the first man. "How does it feel to freeze to death?"

"It's very uncomfortable at first," says the second man. "You get the shakes, and you get pains in all your fingers and toes. But eventually, it's a very calm way to go. You get numb and you kind of drift off, as if you're sleeping. How about you, how did you die?"

"I had a heart attack," says the first man. "You see, I knew my wife was cheating on me, so one day I showed up at home unexpectedly. I ran up to the bedroom, and found her alone, knitting. I ran down to the basement, but no one was hiding there. I ran up to the second floor, but no one was hiding there, either. I ran as fast as I could to the attic, and just as I got there, I had a massive heart attack and died."

The second man shakes his head. "That's so ironic," he says.

"What do you mean?" asks the first man.

"If you had only stopped to look in the freezer, we'd both still be alive."

· P E A R L Y G A T E S ·

 Two men

Outside the Pearly Gates

Two men compare death stories.

The Scotch Wizard

A man walks into a bar and orders Smith & Smith 12-year-old scotch, a rare whiskey. Figuring the man wouldn't know any better, the bartender pours a glass of the house scotch.

The man takes one sip and spits the scotch out. "This is clearly some cheap house brand," says the man. "I specifically ordered Smith & Smith 12-year-old scotch."

The bartender, pissed off about being caught, pours a glass of Johnnie Walker and serves it.

The man takes one sip and spits the scotch out. "This is Johnnie Walker, and while it is a fine scotch, it is not what I ordered. I ordered Smith & Smith 12-year-old scotch."

The bartender, just to see how good he is, pours a glass of Smith & Smith 10-year-old scotch and serves it to the man.

The man takes one sip and spits the scotch out. "I see you've finally found some Smith & Smith, but my good man, this is 10-year-old scotch, as any idiot could taste. I ordered 12-year-old scotch."

A drunk who's been listening to the whole thing hands him a full glass. "Here, buddy," says the drunk, "taste this."

The man takes one sip, and spits it out. "This is piss!" says the man.

"One for one," the drunk says. "Now, how old am I?"

· B A R R O O M ·

A bartender, a connoisseur, a drunk

A bar

A snob demonstrates his unique talent.

The Missing Music

During the intermission of a performance of Beethoven's Ninth Symphony, the conductor grabs his assistant in a panic and tells him that he has noticed that the last few pages of his sheet music are missing. After a few moments of thinking, the assistant realizes that the missing pages were accidentally locked in the storage room. He assures the conductor that by the time they are needed, they'll be on the conductor's music stand.

"They'd better be," says the conductor. "And didn't I tell you to watch the bass players? I see that they're over in the corner, drinking again." With that, he heads back to the stage.

The assistant goes over to the bass players, and pours enough coffee down their throats to get them back to their seats in the orchestra. As the curtain rises for the rest of the symphony, he goes looking for the security guard, who can open the storage room.

With no time to spare, he finds the guard and hurries him to the locked room.

"What's all the panic about?" asks the guard.

"Well," says the assistant, "it's the bottom of the ninth, the score is tied, and the bassists are loaded!"

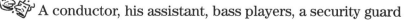

• G R O A N E R •

 A conductor, his assistant, bass players, a security guard

A symphony hall

Drunken bassists and lost music confound a conductor.

The Old Speed Demon

An elderly couple is pulled over for speeding on a country highway. The cop who pulled them over comes to the driver's window, and he says to the old man behind the wheel, "Sir, do you realize you were doing 75 in a 55?"

"Oh, no, sir," says the old man. "That can't be. I never drive over the speed limit."

The old lady sitting next to him, his wife, says, "Ha! Officer, my husband is a speed demon. I'm surprised you didn't clock him at 90!" Her husband just glares at her.

As the cop writes the ticket, he says, "Sir, I've noticed you're not wearing a seat belt. I'm going to have to write you up for that, too."

"But, sir," the old man says, "I *had* it on, but as you were walking toward the car, I took it off to get my wallet out."

"Officer," his wife says, "he's a damned liar. He *never* wears it, and I'm always telling him he should."

The old man can't take this. He turns to his wife and shouts, "God damnit, woman! What's wrong with you?"

The cop leans in a bit and asks the woman, "Ma'am, is your husband always this abusive?"

"Oh, no, sir," she says. "Only when he's been drinking."

• GENERAL •

 An old couple, a cop

 The side of a highway

An old woman rats on her husband.

Sex and Ginger Snaps

One day, a man comes home from work to find his wife very upset. "Honey, what is it?" he asks. "Did something bad happen during little Timmy's first day of school?"

His wife says, "I'm so mad I can barely speak. Do you know what your son said when he got home today?"

The man says, "Please, honey, calm down and just tell me. Whatever it is, we can make it better."

She composes herself and says, "Your son came home today, and when I asked him what he did during his first day of school, he said, 'I ate ginger snaps and screwed the girls all day.'"

The husband's jaw drops. "That's just not right," he says, going right for the frying pan.

The wife, in a panic, says, "Oh my God, honey. I mean, I'm upset too, but we can't hit him with a frying pan!"

"Who's gonna hit him with a frying pan?" the husband asks.

"Well, what are you doing with it, then?" the wife says, staring at her husband, dumbfounded.

"I'm gonna fry him up a steak," the husband says. "You can't expect a boy to screw all day on ginger snaps."

· B A W D Y ·

 A woman, her husband, their son

 A family's home

 A couple radically disagrees on punishment.

The Revolutionary Birthing Pain Machine

A man and a woman are in the delivery room, awaiting the birth of their first child. The labor has been slow going, lasting for hours. The wife, in great agony, asks the doctor, "Can you do something about the pain?"

"Well," says the doctor, "I'm hesitant to recommend this, but there's an experimental device that transfers the pain of birth, by degrees, from the mother to the father. We've only just gotten this device in the hospital, and haven't tested it yet. It would be risky, and I'm afraid the hospital couldn't be held responsible for any side effects."

The husband says, "Whatever it takes at this point, Doc, just help my wife."

The doctor attaches a few electrodes to the wife and explains that the pain is transferred through the air. "This process can get pretty severe in a hurry. How much pain do you think you can handle?" he asks the husband.

Bracing himself in his chair, the husband says, "Give me 25 percent of her pain."

The doctor turns a dial, and the wife relaxes a little. The husband relaxes his grip on the arms of the chair and says, "That's not so bad."

A while later, the wife is again in great pain. The husband says, "Give me 50 percent of her pain," and the doctor turns

the dial. The wife relaxes a little, and the husband, who doesn't seem all that fazed, says, "That's still not so bad."

By now a number of doctors have gathered in the delivery room and watch in amazement as the machine works.

As hard labor begins, the wife screams in obvious agony. She turns to face her husband and pleads with him to take more of her pain.

"Give me 75 percent of her pain!" the husband says, and the doctor turns the dial. Clearly, she's still in some pain, but the husband is doing fine. "Give me *all* of her pain!" says the husband, still in good shape, and the doctor turns the dial all the way. The wife relaxes, and has the baby with ease and no more pain. The doctor removes the electrodes from the husband as the assembled physicians hail the machine as a miracle of modern science.

Everything goes well for the family, until they bring the baby home and find the mailman dead on the lawn.

• G E N E R A L •

A wife, a husband, a doctor, a mailman

A delivery room

A revolutionary machine kills the mailman.

The Hooker's Offer

Cheapskate Bob and his two friends are drinking at the bar when a hooker walks in and struts over to them. "I've had a great night," she tells them, "and I'm in a *very* generous mood. I'll make you guys an offer. I'll do anything you want for $10—as long as you can say it to me in three words."

Bob's first friend wastes no time. Holding out a $10 bill, he whispers three words in her ear. "Okay," she says, "but we'll have to go in the back room for that. They still don't allow that sort of thing in public."

When they come out 10 minutes later, Bob's other friend is waiting with his $10 bill. He whispers three words in her ear, and they go to the back room.

When they come out 20 minutes later, Bob is ready with his $10 bill, much to his friends' surprise. Before handing it to the hooker, he asks her, "You'll do *anything* for $10?"

"Anything, sugar," she says.

"Okay," he says, handing her the money. "Paint my house."

• BAWDY / BARROOM •

Cheapskate Bob, his friends, a hooker

A bar

A hooker does anything for $10.

The Pope and
the Lawyer

The Pope dies and goes straight to heaven, where St. Peter is waiting for him at the Pearly Gates. While he's waiting to be processed, he strikes up a conversation with another newly deceased man, who was a lawyer. St. Peter summons them both through the Gates and says, "These ten angels will show you men to your new heavenly dwellings."

The Pope, the lawyer, and the angels walk together for a while, and then split up. One angel leads the Pope to a small, sparsely furnished hut in a crowded section of heaven, while the other nine angels lead the lawyer up to the top of a majestic mountain, where he is shown to his private penthouse suite, complete with Jacuzzi and personal servants.

For a few weeks, the Pope says nothing in complaint. Finally, he goes to St. Peter and says, "I do not wish to seem ungrateful or self-ish, but I cannot understand why I, a man who has done God's work on earth, am shown such a humble reward while a common lawyer is treated like royalty."

"Look, Pope," St. Peter says, "we're all very proud of you and happy to have you here, but to be frank, heaven is full of Popes—you're nobody special here. But this guy is the first lawyer we've ever had."

• L A W Y E R / P E A R L Y   G A T E S •

The Pope, a lawyer, angels, St. Peter

The Pearly Gates, heaven

God snubs a Pope and rewards a lawyer.

Paying for Golf

Once a year, three men get together for an expensive day of golf. At the end of their most expensive golf day ever, one man says, "You know, we really ought to do this more often than once a year."

The second man disagrees. "Do you have any idea what this costs me?"

The first man says, "Yes, the same as it costs us. But you can afford it."

The second man shakes his head again. "I'm not talking about the actual day. I'm talking about how much I have to spend to get my wife to stop complaining about how much I spend on this day. This year, shutting her up is going to cost me a fur coat!"

The third man speaks up. "That's all? A fur coat? It's going to cost me at least a week in Bermuda!"

The first man can't believe what he's hearing. "You guys just don't know how to talk to your wives," he says.

"Oh yeah?" the second one says. "How do you keep your wife from complaining about the money you spend on our golf outings?"

"It's easy. On this day every year, I wake my wife up early in the morning and I say 'Well? Should I go play golf, or would you rather spend the day making love?' To which she always replies, 'You'd better take a sweater, it looks chilly out.'"

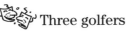

Three golfers

A golf course

Different strategies for golf escapes are discussed.

Lawyer's Pet Trick

Three men and their dogs appear on a comedy/talk show that features pet tricks. The first man introduces himself as an accountant and explains what his dog will do: "This is my dog, CPA. He will hop up on that table, count the number of beers, and bark out that number." Sure enough, CPA hops up on the table and barks 16 times, once for every beer on the table. The audience applauds.

The second man introduces himself as a mathematician and explains what his dog will do: "This is my dog, Slide Rule. He will hop up on that table, count the number of beers, and bark out the square root of that number." Sure enough, Slide Rule jumps up on the table, sees the 16 beers, and barks four times. The audience applauds even louder.

The third man introduces himself as a lawyer and introduces his dog, Litigant. Litigant jumps up on the table, drinks all 16 beers, screws the other two dogs, and takes the rest of the day off.

• LAWYER •

An accountant, a mathematician, a lawyer

A comedy/talk TV show

A lawyer's dog stays in character.

The Captain and the Camel

The French Foreign Legion transferred a captain to a new command in the desert. During his first inspection of his base, he notices an old camel hitched to a post behind the mess tent. He asks the sergeant showing him around what the camel is kept there for.

"Well, sir," the sergeant says, "as you know, we have 250 men on this base, and no women. And, sir, sometimes the men have . . . *urges.* That's why we have the camel, sir."

The captain says, "I can't say as I condone this, but I do understand about urges, so the camel can stay."

About a month later, the captain starts having a real problem with his own urges, and he asks the sergeant to bring the camel to his tent. Putting a stool behind the camel, the captain stands up on it, pulls down his pants, and has sex with the camel. When he's done, he asks the sergeant, "Is that how the men do it?"

"Uh, no, sir," the sergeant replies. "They usually just ride the camel into town."

· B A W D Y ·

 A captain, a sergeant, an old camel

 A desert base

Sex with a camel

The Dejected Songwriter

A man walks into a bar and orders a shot of whiskey. After throwing that back, he has another. And another. Three or four shots later, the bartender says to him, "Look, I know it's none of my business, but are you okay?"

"No," says the man, "I'm not. Today I had my life's work rejected for the twentieth time."

"What do you do?" asks the bartender.

"I write songs," says the man, "and I've had them rejected by twenty different record companies, counting today. I think they're pretty good, but no one else seems to think so."

To cheer the man up, the bartender says, "Well, would you like to play one for me?" He points to the bar's piano.

"You would?" says the man, flattered. "Why, of course."

Fully expecting to hate what he hears, the bartender sits down next to the piano, prepared to lie and tell him how good his song is. As the man begins playing, it becomes clear that the bartender won't have to lie, as the music is beautiful. By the time the song is over, a good crowd has appeared, and they applaud loudly.

The bartender buys the man a drink and says, "I honestly can't figure out how anyone could reject that beautiful song. What's it called?"

"That one," says the man, "is called, 'I Love You So Much I Could Shit.'"

• BARROOM •

 A songwriter, a bartender

 A bar

A songwriter can't title songs to save his life.

The Limbless Woman
at the Beach

Walking along the beach, a man looks out over the ocean, and then notices a young lady on the sand up ahead. As he walks closer to her, he sees that she has no arms and no legs, and that she's crying quietly. "What's the matter?" he asks.

"I'm very lonely," the girl tells him. "Because I have no arms and no legs, I've never been held tightly."

Feeling sorry for her, the man picks her up from the sand and embraces her. After a while, he puts her down and starts to walk away. He hasn't gotten five steps when he hears her crying again.

"What's the matter?" he asks her.

"Because I have no arms and no legs, I've never been kissed passionately," she says.

With that, the man picks her up from the sand and kisses her passionately for a while. He hasn't gotten five steps when she cries again.

"*Now* what's the matter," he asks her, but she won't answer. "Please tell me," he says.

"Well," she says, "it's just that because I have no arms and no legs, I've, well, I've never been screwed."

With that, he shrugs, picks her up from the sand, throws her into the ocean and says, "Now you're screwed."

· B A W D Y ·

 A man, a limbless woman

 The beach

 A limbless woman gets her wish.

The Little Blackmailer

A married woman locks her son in the closet whenever her lover comes over. One day, in the middle of having sex with her lover, she hears her husband's car in the driveway. She pushes her lover into the closet with the boy.

"It sure is dark in here," the boy says to the lover, who agrees.

"Hey mister," the boy goes on. "Wanna buy my baseball?"

"No, thanks," says the lover.

"I think you really should buy my baseball," the boy says, and the lover catches on that he's being blackmailed.

"Okay, how much?" he asks the boy.

"Twenty-five bucks," the boy says, and the lover pays him.

The next week, it happens again: the lover is thrown in the closet with the boy.

"It sure is dark in here," the boy says to the lover, who agrees.

"Hey mister," the boy goes on. "Wanna buy my baseball glove?"

The lover doesn't even argue. He hands the boy $50.

A week later, the boy's father says, "Hey, son, let's go have a catch." The boy explains that he sold his glove and ball for $75.

"Son, that's robbery! I'm taking you to church so you can confess your sin."

Once inside the confessional, the boy says to the priest, "It sure is dark in here," to which the priest responds, "What, now you want to sell me your *bat*?"

· B A W D Y ·

 A little boy, his father, his mother's lover

 In the closet, then in the confessional

A boy blackmails a priest.

The
British Amputee and
the Nazi

A British flyer is captured behind enemy lines during World War II. Badly wounded, he is taken to a Nazi hospital, where he is alternately treated and interrogated.

"Major," a Nazi soldier says to him, "I am afraid ve vill haff to amputate your right leg. Ziss is most regrettable, and my commandant vould like to know if zere is anysing ve can do to make your stay here more comfortable."

"No, there isn't," says the major. "But I would like to request that my leg be buried in British soil."

"I vill see vhat I can do."

The next day, after the leg is removed, the Nazi comes to see the major in the hospital ward and says, "Ve haff made arrangements to drop your leg over Britain on ze next bombing raid. Iz ziss satisfactory?"

"Yes," says the major.

"Unfortunately," the Nazi continues, "ze doctors have declared zat your injuries are more severe zan ve thought, and ve now haff to amputate your left leg."

"I would like to request," the major says, "that my left leg also be buried in England."

"I vill see vhat I can do."

The next day, after the second operation, the Nazi comes to see the major, and says, "Ve haff dropped your right leg over Britain, and haff made arrangements to drop your left leg on ze next bombing raid. Is ziss satisfactory?"

"Yes," says the major.

"Unfortunately," the Nazi continues, "though our doctors are ze best trained in ze world, zey have not been successful in zere efforts to save your right arm. Ve now haff to amputate your right arm."

"I'd like that buried in England as well."

"I vill see vhat I can do."

The next day, after the third operation, the Nazi comes to see the major, and says, "Ve haff dropped your left leg over Britain, and haff made arrangements to drop your right arm on ze next bombing raid. Is ziss satisfactory?"

"Yes," says the major.

"Unfortunately," the Nazi continues, "ze bad news continues. Ze doctors haff informed me zat zere is nothing more zey can do, and ve now haff to amputate your left arm."

"I'd like it buried with the rest."

"I vill see vhat I can do."

The next day the Nazi comes in, very angry. "You have been tricking me, Major, and I vill not allow it to continue. Ve vill not be dropping your left arm over Britain."

"But, why?" asks the major.

"I haff discussed your requests vis my superiors," the Nazi says. "Ve sink you are trying to escape."

· G R O A N E R ·

A British major, a Nazi soldier

A Nazi hospital

Escape by amputation

The Old Sperm Donor

A 92-year-old man goes to the sperm bank, where he tells the receptionist that he would like to make a donation. "I'm sorry, sir," she tells him, "but at 92 you're just way too old to donate sperm."

"Listen here, young lady," the old man says. "I've led a full and active life, and I'm as fit today as I was at 30. In fact, I even bench press twice my weight."

To get rid of him, she gives in. Handing him a beaker with a cap on it, she points to a room at the end of the hall. "When you're done," she tells him, "please come out and see me."

A half hour goes by, and the old man has not come out of the room, so the nurse knocks on the door. "Are you okay?" she asks.

"Well I'm having a little trouble," comes the reply from behind the door. "I've tried it with my left hand, I've tried it with my right hand, and I've tried it between my knees," the old man says, "but nothing seems to work."

"At your age," the nurse says, "I'm not surprised."

"Okay, smartass," the old man says, "how would *you* get the cap off?"

· B A W D Y ·

 An old man, a young nurse

 A sperm bank

An old man struggles with a sperm donation.

The Teacher's Hard Questions

Miss Jones says to her class one day, "Now I know that summer vacation is only two weeks away, and you are all having a hard time paying attention. So I'll make you a deal: Every day this week, I'll ask you a question. If anyone can answer it, I'll give you all next week off. Today's Monday, so here's the question: How many grains of sand are in the Sahara desert?"

Not one of the third graders raises a hand.

On Tuesday, Miss Jones says, "Here's today's question: How many drops of water are in the Atlantic Ocean?"

Not one of the third graders raises a hand.

On Wednesday, Miss Jones asks how many stars there are in the sky, and on Thursday she asks exactly how many people live in China.

Disgusted with these impossible questions, Little Eddie wakes up early Friday morning and steals his father's glass eye.

In school that day, Miss Jones says, Today's question is . . ." But before she can continue, Eddie takes the glass eye out of his pocket and rolls it loudly up the aisle, where it bounces off Miss Jones's desk. She picks it up and says, "Okay, who's the funnyman with the glass eye?"

Eddie says, "Sammy Davis Jr.! See you in September!"

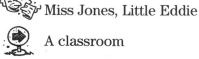

·CLASSROOM·

Miss Jones, Little Eddie

A classroom

Little Eddie uses a glass eye to outsmart the teacher.

The Veteran's Medical Problem

A soldier, just back from Vietnam, goes to his doctor about an embarrassing infection in his penis. It's been steadily turning a nasty shade of green, and he doesn't know what to do about it. His doctor, unsure of the cause, but concerned about a possible spread to other parts of the body, tells the soldier that he should have his penis amputated.

The soldier quickly goes for a second opinion, but the next doctor says the same thing: The safest thing is to cut off the penis. The soldier asks the doctor, "Do you know anyone who might be able to tell me what is causing this before I have to take such radical action?"

The doctor says, "There is an Asian doctor up the road who seems to recognize a lot of strange afflictions in Vietnam vets. Perhaps you should see him."

The soldier does, and the Asian doctor quickly diagnoses the problem. "Very rare venereal disease," says the doctor. "I see it all the time in soldiers."

"But tell me, Doc," the soldier says, "do I have to have my penis cut off?"

The doctor laughs. "Of course not. Wait two or three days. It'll fall off by itself!"

· B A W D Y ·

A soldier, two American doctors, an Asian doctor

Various doctors' offices

A man considers amputation of a critical organ.

The Three Stages of Sex

Just before his son's wedding, a father is giving last-minute advice about married life to his son. "You all set with sex, son?" "Yeah, Pop, I got that covered," the son says with a smile.

"Okay, smart guy," the father says, "what are the three stages of sex in marriage?"

"You got me," says the son.

The father says, "You have honeymoon sex, holiday sex, and hallway sex. Honeymoon sex is what you have for the first few years; you can't wait to have sex with each other and you do it at every available opportunity. In a few years, you start to have holiday sex."

"What's that?" asks the son.

"That's when you don't do it so often anymore—you wait for special occasions like birthdays or anniversaries or holidays to have

sex. After 20 years or so, you start to have hallway sex."

"What's *that*?" asks the son.

"That's when you pass each other in the hallway and say, 'Fuck you.'"

· B A W D Y ·

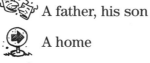 A father, his son

A home

A father explains the realities of marital sex.

Dueling Limos

Bob and Frank go shopping for new cars. Bob buys a Mercedes limousine and Frank buys a Cadillac limousine. A few days later, they pull up alongside each other at a stoplight.

"Nice car," Bob says to Frank, "but is it loaded?"

"Yeah, it's loaded," Frank says.

"Gotta phone?" Bob asks.

"Yeah, I gotta phone."

"Gotta television?"

"Yeah, I gotta television," Frank says.

"That's nice. You gotta bed?"

Frank laughs. "No, I don't have a bed. Yours has a bed?"

Bob says, "Oh, yeah. It's great." And with that, his car pulls away.

Frank is furious that he's been shown up. He goes to the Cadillac dealership and demands that a bed be installed.

A week later, he picks up his Cadillac, complete with a new bed. He has his driver take him out searching for Bob. Finally, they see the Mercedes pulled over to the side of the road with the flashers on.

Frank knocks on the window, but there is no answer. He pounds on the window, and eventually Bob rolls it down and says, "What? What do you want?"

"Hi, Bob," Frank says, "I just wanted to tell you about my new bed."

Bob says, "You pulled me out of the shower to tell me that?"

• GENERAL •

Bob, Frank

On the street

 Two limos have more options than a Winnebago.

The
Proctologist's Discovery

A young medical student, hoping to get a little extra studying done for his proctology exam, breaks into the medical lab late at night. He pulls out a few cadavers, and notices right away that they each have corks stuck in their anuses. He removes the cork from one, and out of the orifice comes a voice singing, "On the road again, just can't wait to get on the road again." He sticks the cork back in. When he uncorks another cadaver, the anus starts singing, "Mamas, don't let your babies grow up to be cowboys."

He's shocked by his discovery. Certain he's stumbled onto an amazing medical find, he runs to the dean of the medical school's home, and wakes him up.

"What is it?" the dean demands.

"Sir, please come with me," the student says. "You're gonna have to experience this for yourself."

At the lab, the student says, "I know it was wrong to break in like this, but I only wanted to be more prepared for my exam. Just look what I found!" With that, he pulls the corks out, and the voices come again, each singing their respective song. "Isn't that amazing?" the student asks.

"What's so amazing?" the dean says, annoyed. "Any asshole can sing country."

· G R O A N E R ·

 A medical student, his dean

A deserted medical lab

Cadavers possess strange musical talents.

Joe Gets a
Papal Embrace

Joe is visiting St. Peter's Square in Vatican City when he hears
that the Pope is inside the church, greeting visitors personally.
He rushes to get on line.

While he's waiting, he sees a raggedy, foul-smelling bum in line
ahead of him. Joe sees the Pope greet the man with an embrace
rather than the handshake he'd been giving everyone else. "Boy,
would that be something," Joe muses. "I wonder how I could get the
Pope to hug me so that I could tell the folks back home about it . . ."

Soon enough, Joe comes up with a plan. He gets out of line
and goes into the square. There, he tears his clothes, rolls around
on the pavement, and rubs dirt and pigeon droppings on himself
until he resembles (and smells like) the bum that the Pope
hugged. He goes back inside and returns to the line.

Sure enough, when his turn comes, the Pope doesn't just shake
his hand, he pulls Joe to him in an embrace. And there, arms around
each other and cheek to cheek, the Pope whispers in Joe's ear, "I
thought I made it very clear to you before, get your smelly ass out
of here."

·R E L I G I O N·

 Joe, the Pope, a bum

St. Peter's

Joe gets booted out of St. Peter's by the Pope.

40

The Farmer's House of Sod

A farmer builds himself a home completely out of Kentucky bluegrass, and uses the second and third floors for his impressive collection of the chairs of kings, purchased from kingdoms around the world. The chairs are all ornate and all beautiful, and the farmer spends much of his time taking excellent care of them.

One day, the farmer decides that it is time to fertilize the bluegrass that makes up the structure of the house, and he moves all of his precious chairs to the attic. He carefully spreads fertilizer on the third floor, and then waters it. Satisfied, he goes to the second floor and repeats the process. He fertilizes the family quarters on the first floor, and finally goes down to the basement to finish his job.

While he's down there, there is a tremendous creaking. The weight of the chairs is too much for the attic floorboards, and the chairs come crashing down. They crash through the third, second, and first floors, and crush the poor farmer to death.

The moral of the story: People in grass houses shouldn't stow thrones.

• G R O A N E R •

A farmer

A grass farmhouse

A farmer discovers the weakness of sod.

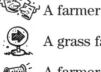

The Shipwrecked Man and the Wild Pig

A man and his dog are shipwrecked on a small desert island. After months of isolation, the man misses sex so much that he starts thinking about making love to the only other inhabitant other than his dog on the island, a wild pig.

One day, he gives in to his urges and walks over to where the pig is sleeping. Before the man can do anything, the dog goes nuts, barking at the man and biting at his legs. As soon as the man moves away from the pig, the dog quiets down.

This goes on for months: The man attempts to make love to the pig, and the dog goes nuts, not allowing the man near the pig.

Finally, the man gives up.

Some time later, another ship is wrecked on the reef, and the only survivor is a beautiful woman, who washes up on shore. The man thanks God for His generosity.

When she wakes up, the man says to her, "You are safe. I will make sure that you eat, and that you are protected from the storms."

Grateful, she says, "Is there anything I can do for you? Anything at all?"

"Yes," he says with an expectant smile. "Could you watch the dog for a while?"

· B A W D Y ·

 A man, a dog, a wild pig, a beautiful woman

 A desert island

 Attempted sex with a pig

The Clever Counterman

Walking up to the counter at his local deli, a man orders half a head of lettuce. The counterman takes the order and walks to the back, where his manager is working on the books. "Can you believe this?" the counterman says. "Some jerk just ordered half a head of lettuce."

As soon as he's said it, the counterman notices that the customer has followed him and is standing right behind him. Thinking fast, the counterman adds, "But this nice man has ordered the other half, so there's no problem."

The manager is impressed with the counterman's quick thinking, and later in the day offers him a job opening a new deli outlet in Canada.

"Canada?" says the counterman incredulously. "All they have in Canada is whores and hockey players."

The manager, furious, says, "My wife is from Canada."

The counterman, acting very interested, says, "Oh, yeah? What team does she play for?"

• *G E N E R A L* •

A counterman, a deli manager, a customer

A deli

Insulting Canadians

Mike Tyson and the Pope's Blessing

The following is what's commonly referred to as a visual joke. Telling it requires the common "blessing" hand gesture. With the right hand—index and middle fingers almost straight pointing upward—motion up, motion down, motion to the left, and to the right.

Mike Tyson and Don King are visiting St. Peter's in Vatican City. Tyson is eating pistachios and dropping the shells on the floor of the church. King says, "Champ, you can't make a mess like this—this is the Vatican! See that man over there? That's the Pope!"

"I'm the baddest man in boxing," Tyson says. "I do what I want, where I want."

Seeing the Pope approaching, King goes over to a pew and sits down, hoping not to be seen. From the pew, he sees the Pope bless Tyson. *(Do the blessing gesture, as discussed above.)*

When the Pope walks away, King runs over to Tyson and says, "I can't believe that the Pope blessed you!"

"He didn't bless me," Tyson says. "He said, 'I want you *(start the blessing—point up)* to clean up this shit *(point down)*, take the clown with the hair *(point left)*, and *(point right)* get out.'"

• RELIGION/GENERAL •

 Mike Tyson, Don King, the Pope

St. Peter's

The Pope joins the ranks of Tyson-bashers.

The Cannibal Chief and the Guy from New York

An Englishman, a Frenchman, and a guy from New York are on safari in the deepest, darkest jungle when they're captured by a vicious cannibal tribe. The chief of the tribe says to them, "We will eat your flesh, we will grind your bones into powder, we will drink soup from your skulls. Then, we will dry your skin and use it to line our canoes. But we are not heartless; you may choose how you die."

The Englishman says, "I'll take the pistol, if you please." He puts the gun to his head, says "God save the Queen!" and pulls the trigger.

The Frenchman says, "I will take ze sword." He puts the tip of the sword under his chest, says "Vive la France!" and falls forward onto the blade.

The guy from New York thinks for a minute, then says, "Gimme a fork." He takes the fork and starts stabbing himself all over his body, causing hundreds of tiny, bloody wounds. As it becomes apparent that the guy intends to keep this up until he bleeds to death, the chief says, "What are you doing?" The guy from New York says, "I'm fuckin' up ya canoe, ya bastard."

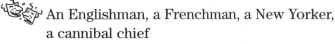

• GENERAL •

 An Englishman, a Frenchman, a New Yorker, a cannibal chief

 A tribal camp in the deep jungle

Three men choose how to die.

The
FBI Loyalty Test

The FBI is down to three candidates for a spot in its Washington, D.C., office; a 25-year-old, a 35-year-old, and a 45-year-old. Each is scheduled for a final interview on the same day, two hours apart.

The 25-year-old comes in first, and, as requested, he brings his wife with him. She sits in the waiting room while he goes in to meet with two agents. "You are a great candidate," one agent tells him. "In fact, you tested so well that we're going to offer you this job on the spot, provided you prove your unquestioning loyalty to us, and your ability to take even the harshest orders."

"What must I do?" he asks. "Name it."

"Take this gun," one agent says, handing him a revolver, "go into the waiting room, and shoot your wife dead."

"You guys are crazy!" the candidate says. "I'm not going to kill my wife just for a job! I *love* her . . . we're going to have a baby soon. Good day, gentlemen." With that, he leaves.

Two hours later, the 35-year-old comes in, leaving his wife in the waiting room while he goes in to talk to the agents. "You know," one of them says, "we don't usually let agents start careers here over the age of 30. But you're in terrific shape, you're smart as hell . . . frankly, the job is yours, if you can prove your unquestioning loyalty to us, and your ability to take even the harshest orders." The agent tells the candidate to take the revolver and shoot his wife dead.

"Hmm . . ." the man says, clearly thinking about this. "Well . . . oh, I'm sorry, I just can't. I mean, no offense—I really wanted to be an agent—but I'm kind of fond of my wife, and we have small children at home who would miss their mom, so I can't do it. Thanks anyway," he says, on his way out.

Two hours later, the final candidate comes in, leaving his wife in the waiting room. "I have to say," one agent tells him, "that we've never considered offering this job to a man of your age. But you tested through the roof, so we're going to make an exception, provided you can prove your unquestioning loyalty to us, and your ability to take even the harshest orders." The agent offers the 45-year-old the revolver, and tells him what he must do.

Without hesitation, the final candidate gets up, takes the gun, and leaves the room. From the waiting area, the agents hear a loud BAM! followed by five more, in rapid succession: BAM! BAM! BAM-BAMBAM! Then they hear a WHACK! followed by a few more: WHACK! WHACK! WHACKWHACKWHACK!

The candidate comes back into the room, completely disheveled. As he's tucking his shirt back in and straightening his tie, an agent says, "What the hell was *that* all about? What was all that noise?"

The candidate says, "Oh, that. I had to beat her to death with a chair. Some idiot put blanks in the gun."

· G E N E R A L ·

 Three job candidates, two FBI agents

A conference room

Three men are asked to kill their wives.

The Philanderer and the Talcum Powder

A man calls his wife and tells her he's going to be working late. As soon as he hangs up the phone, he goes to the local singles bar, where he meets a beautiful young woman. He buys her drinks, he takes her dancing, then he goes to her place and makes passionate love to her, and falls asleep.

At one o'clock in the morning, he wakes up. In a panic, he asks the woman for some talcum powder, which he rubs on his hands.

His wife is waiting when he walks in the door a short time later, and she says, "Where the hell have you been?"

"Okay, honey, I'll tell you the truth. I went to the local singles bar, and met a beautiful young woman. I bought her drinks, I took her dancing, and then I made love to her and fell asleep."

"Let me see your hands," his wife says. He shows her.

"You liar," she says, "you've been bowling again."

• GENERAL / BAWDY •

A man, a single woman, the man's wife

A singles bar, the woman's home, the home

A man's futile attempt to confess to adultery

The Lone Ranger Goes Solo

The Lone Ranger and Tonto are riding north through a canyon when they see a tribe of Native Americans coming toward them. "They don't look friendly, Tonto," says the Lone Ranger.

"These are Apaches," says Tonto. "Angry over treatment by soldiers. They are out for blood."

They turn around only to notice another tribe coming at them from the south. "They don't look happy, either," remarks the masked man.

"These are Sioux," says Tonto. "Angry over treatment by settlers. They, too, are out for blood."

They ride toward the setting sun and soon see yet another tribe, coming from the west. The Lone Ranger is worried. "Who are they?"

"These are Cherokee," says Tonto. "Angry about forced settlement on reservations. They are also out for blood."

The Lone Ranger and Tonto turn to ride to the east and soon see one more tribe coming at them. They are effectively boxed in. Tonto explains, "These are collected war councils. Angry about *everything*."

Realizing they don't have a chance of getting out of their predicament alive, the Lone Ranger says to Tonto, "Well, at least I'll go down with my trusted friend at my side."

Tonto says, "Are you talking to me, white man?"

• G E N E R A L •

The Lone Ranger, Tonto, tribes of Native Americans

A canyon out West

The Lone Ranger's trusty companion comes to his senses.

The Third Grade Stress Test

Miss Jones, the third grade teacher, gives her class an assignment. "Tonight, boys and girls, I want you to go home and see what types of things you and your families need to have in order to avoid stress. I want you each to choose one thing and draw a picture of it for tomorrow."

The next day, Miss Jones has the children stand up one by one and show their pictures to the class. She points to one little girl's picture and says, "Susie, I see that you've drawn a stack of money. How does not having money cause stress?"

"Well," says Susie, "my mommy always tells my daddy that there's not enough money to pay the bills, and they both feel stress about it."

"Good," Miss Jones says. "Tommy, you've drawn a television. Why?"

"We only have one television in our house," Tommy explains. "My sisters fight with my dad over who gets to watch what. Because we don't have more televisions, my sisters feel a lot of stress."

"That's great," Miss Jones says. She looks at Little Eddie's picture. "Eddie, I see you've drawn a dot. Can you explain that to us?"

Eddie shakes his head, and says, "That's not a dot, that's a period. My sister hasn't had two in a row and my whole *family* is stressed."

• C L A S S R O O M / B A W D Y •

 Miss Jones, Susie, Tommy, Little Eddie

 A classroom

Little Eddie reveals the importance of his sister's menstrual cycle.

The Miracle Headache Cure

A man goes to the doctor with a splitting headache. "Doc," he says, "I've tried everything from aspirin to prescription pain killers, and nothing cures this. I'm desperate, Doc! You've gotta help me. I feel like I'm gonna die."

The doctor does every test he can think of, finds nothing wrong, and says to the man, "All I can tell you is that when I get a headache like that, I go straight home to my wife. Wherever she is in the house, whatever she's doing, I lead her into the bedroom. I make passionate love to her for a few hours, making sure to please her as much as I can, and that always seems to cure it."

The next day, the man comes back with relief written all over his face. "Doc! You cured me!" he says. "I did just what you said and had great sex for hours . . . she loved it, and before I knew it, the headache was gone. I'm a completely new man. You're a genius! And by the way, Doc . . ."

"Yes?"

"You have a beautiful home."

· BAWDY ·

 A doctor, his patient

 A doctor's office

A doctor and his patient share the same headache cure.

The Pharmacist and the Big Box

A man walks into a pharmacy, and asks the pharmacist for a large box of condoms. No sooner has the pharmacist handed the box over than the man starts laughing hysterically. The man pays for the condoms and walks out of the store, still laughing.

"Boy, was that strange," the pharmacist says to the stock boy.

"Yes, sir, it was," the stock boy agrees.

The next day, the same man comes in to the pharmacy, and asks for the same thing: a large box of condoms. This time, the man starts laughing even *before* the box is handed over. After he pays and leaves, the pharmacist says to the stock boy, "Boy, that was strange." The stock boy agrees.

When the same thing happens the next day—the same request for a large box of condoms, followed by gales of laughter—the pharmacist waits until the man has left before saying to the stock boy, "Son, I'm dying of curiosity. I want you to follow that man and tell me anything you can about him; where he works, where he lives. Whatever." The stock boy goes.

Five hours later, the stock boy comes back. "Did you lose him?" the pharmacist asks.

"No, sir," says the boy. "He's been at your house all day."

• B A W D Y •

 A pharmacist, a stock boy, a customer

A pharmacy

A customer gets the last laugh on a pharmacist.

The Engineer in Hell

Upon passing on, an engineer finds himself outside the Pearly Gates. St. Peter spies him on line, and says "Wait a minute; you're an engineer, aren't you? I'm tired of you engineers. You're always screwing things up down on earth with all your inventions and your fancy ideas. You're going to Hell." With that, the engineer is cast down into Hell.

After a few weeks of misery, the engineer says to himself, "Hey, I don't have to suffer like this. I'm an engineer. I'll just make improvements." Within weeks, Hell has air-conditioning, indoor plumbing, nice escalators—all the comforts.

Shortly after the improvements have been made, God happens to call Satan, to see how things are. "Still miserable, I trust?" God says.

"Actually, no," says Satan. "Now that you folks sent us an engineer, things are quite nice in Hell. People are happy to be here. Thanks so much!"

God is furious. "You send that engineer back up here. That was a mistake, sending him to you!" he thunders.

"Nope," says Satan. "You guys sent him; we're keeping him."

God can't believe the insolence. "You send him back, or I'll . . . I'll . . . I'll sue you!"

Satan says, "Yeah, right. And where are *you* gonna find a lawyer?"

• LAWYER / PEARLY GATES •

 An engineer, St. Peter, God, Satan

Heaven, Hell

God and Satan argue over the strength of their legal positions.

The Shipwrecked Lawyer

Three men are shipwrecked: a doctor, a lawyer, and a crewman. As their rowboat drifts aimlessly, they discuss who should attempt to swim the shark-infested waters to shore, in search of help.

"I'll never make it," says the crewman, "not with this gash I got when I fell against the railing of the sinking ship."

The doctor says to the lawyer, "He's right, and he needs constant medical attention so he doesn't slip into a coma. I'm afraid that if I go, he'll die."

"That's it, then," says the lawyer. "I guess I'm the man." He dives into the water, and suddenly the sea is filled with shark fins converging on the spot where he's disappeared beneath the surface. The doctor and the crewman are sure that the lawyer's been ripped to pieces, but moments later he surfaces on the back of a shark, with the other sharks lined up on either side, guiding him in to shore.

A few hours later, he returns in a Coast Guard helicopter, and the doctor and the crewman are rescued. On the trip home, the doctor asks the lawyer, "Why did the sharks do that for you?"

The lawyer says, "Professional courtesy."

· L A W Y E R ·

 A lawyer, a doctor, a crewman

 A lifeboat at sea

 A lawyer gets help from his compatriots.

Young Patrick's Confession

Young Patrick goes into the confessional and says, "Bless me, Father, for I have sinned. I've used the Lord's name in vain, I cheated on my schoolwork, and I've spent time with a loose woman."

The priest says, "Patrick O'Flannery, is that you in my confessional?" The boy tells him it is, and the priest goes on. "Son, you have to come clean about who this girl was. Was it Katie Flaherty?"

Patrick says, "No, Father."

"Well, was it Mary Elizabeth Callahan?"

Patrick says, "No, Father."

"Hmm. Could it have been Margaret Mary Quinn?"

Patrick says, "No, Father."

"Son, tell me: Was it Connie McBride?"

Patrick says, "No, Father . . . and I can't tell you who it was."

The priest sighs, and says, "All right, son. It's between you and God. For that and your other sins, say five Our Fathers and ten Hail Marys. Off you go."

When Patrick gets back to his pew, his friend Tommy says, "What'd you get?"

Patrick says "Five Our Fathers, ten Hail Marys, and four good leads."

· R E L I G I O N ·

Young Patrick and a priest

A confessional

Patrick gets more than he bargains for.

The Mormon Sex Talk

A young Jewish man is nervous about offending his father-in-law-to-be, who is a Mormon. The night before the wedding, he goes to speak with the old man. "Sir," he says, "out of respect for you and your beliefs—and because I am not familiar with any type of Christianity—I wanted to ask you a few questions about what you expect from me."

"You honor me," the old man says. "Please ask."

"Well, I don't want to be indelicate," the young man says, "but we *will* be allowed to consummate this marriage . . ."

The old man laughs. "Of course, my son."

"Should we wait a certain period?" he asks, still nervous.

"Tomorrow is your wedding day. If I were you, I would consummate my marriage tomorrow night!" the old man exclaims.

A little relaxed, the young man presses on. "Should I be on top?"

"If that is what you wish."

"Could she be on top?" the young man asks.

"Of course she can."

"Can we do it standing up?" the young man wonders.

"No," the old man says, "that I must forbid."

"But, why?"

"Because, my son, *that* could lead to dancing . . ."

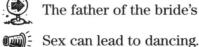

• R E L I G I O N / B A W D Y •

 An elderly father of the bride, a young groom

The father of the bride's house

Sex can lead to dancing.

5 6

The Oprah Argument

Waking up early one morning, a man and his girlfriend make passionate love to each other. Afterward, while he's showering and dressing for work, she lovingly cooks him breakfast. When it's time for him to leave, she walks him to the porch and tenderly kisses him good-bye. They are a vision of domestic tranquillity.

Until he gets home that night. His girlfriend is on the porch once more when he pulls into the driveway, but this time she has her bags packed and is clearly angry.

"What could it possibly be?" he quickly asks her. "What's the matter?"

"I know what you are, you bastard, and I can't believe it!" she tells him.

"Wait a minute," he says. "What's going on here? What have I done?"

She stares at him, angrily. "Do you know what I do when you're at work every day? I watch the talk shows. Well, I was watching *Oprah* today, and I found out what you are. *You* are a *pedophile*," she says.

"Hold on just a minute," he says. "First of all, don't you think *'pedophile'* is an awfully big word for a 12-year-old?"

· B A W D Y ·

 A man, his girlfriend

The front porch of a house

A man tries to calm his Lolita.

5 7

God and Saul Make Pants

Saul Abrams has a little clothing store. Doing poorly, and afraid that he'll have to let his employees go, Saul goes to temple and asks God for help. Suddenly, Saul hears the voice of God, who says, "Make pleated pants."

Saul goes back to the store and starts working feverishly on pleated pants. In a matter of weeks, the store is wildly successful, and pleated pants are all the rage. With his newfound wealth, Saul expands, so that he can give more people work.

Unfortunately, Saul isn't a great businessman, and he expands too much and can't pay his overhead. Sheepishly, he goes back to temple and asks God for more help. Again, Saul hears the voice of God, who says, "Make lapels that aren't so wide."

Saul goes back to the store and starts working feverishly on narrower lapels. In a matter of weeks, the store is once again in the black, and Saul has learned his lesson. After thinking about how to pay homage to God, he goes back to temple.

"God," he says, "I want to show my appreciation for all your blessings, so I've named the store 'Abrams and God.'"

God speaks once more to Saul, and says. "No. Don't use our names, use our occupations. And I get first billing."

"What should I call it?" says Saul. "Lord and Tailor?"

• R E L I G I O N / G R O A N E R •

 God, Saul

Saul's clothing store, a temple

Divine business advice

The Little Man and the Piano

A guy walks into a bar with a box. He opens the box and pulls out a foot-tall man in a tuxedo, as well as a tiny piano. The little man sits down at the little piano and starts playing. The bartender says to the guy, "Say, fella, that's amazing!"

The guy says, "I'll make you a deal. This little man will keep playing if you'll let me drink for free." The bartender quickly agrees.

A few drinks later, the bartender says, "If you don't mind my asking, where'd you find this little man?"

The guy says, "Well, I was walking on a beach, and I found a lamp. When I rubbed it, a genie appeared, and offered to grant me one wish. This is what I got." The man thinks for a moment, and adds, "Hey, I still have the lamp. Would *you* like a wish?"

The bartender eagerly takes the lamp, rubs it, and says to the genie, "I'd like a million bucks." At first, nothing happens. But then, an almost deafening roar starts coming from the one million ducks on the street outside.

The bartender goes back to the guy at the bar and says, "Damn. Your genie must be hard of hearing. I said 'bucks,' not 'ducks.'"

"Of course he's hard of hearing," the guy says. "You don't think I asked for a 12-inch *pianist*, do you?"

• B A R R O O M / G E N I E •

 A man, a bartender, a foot-tall man, a genie

A bar

A deaf genie helps scam drinks.

5 9

Abstinence

Three Catholic couples—an old couple, a middle-aged couple, and a young couple—are about to be excommunicated when their local bishop calls them all into his office and makes them the following offer: "If all of you can abstain from sex for one month, I will let you back in the Church."

One month later, he calls them all back into his office. He turns to the elderly couple and says, "Have you done what I asked?"

The husband replies, "Your Excellency, we haven't had sex in ten years. One month was no problem."

The bishop says, "You're back in the Church," and turns to the middle-aged couple, saying, "Have you done what I asked?"

The husband replies, "Your Excellency, it was tough, but our faith in God and our desire to be good won out."

The bishop says, "You're back in the Church," and turns to the young couple, saying, "Have you done what I asked?"

The husband sighs. "We lasted about two weeks, and then one day my wife was bending over with some groceries, and I just flipped up her skirt, and . . ."

The bishop says, "I'm sorry, but I can't let you back in the Church."

The husband replies, "Don't feel bad, Your Excellency, they're not going to let us back in the A & P, either."

· R E L I G I O N / B A W D Y ·

 A bishop, an older couple, a middle-aged couple, a young couple

A bishop's office

Three couples try to get back in the church.

The Hooker's Perfect Lovers

A man in the first-class section of an airplane notices a beautiful woman sitting across the aisle. She has an expensive fur wrap on the seat next to her, and diamonds everywhere. Clearly, she is very rich.

The man buys a bottle of champagne, and after talking her into joining him for a glass of bubbly, he asks where she got her fortune.

"I'm a prostitute," she says, "and I make $100,000 a night."

"You must be very good at what you do," he says.

"I am," she says. "In fact, I charge some men a million a night."

"Do you ever have sex for free?" he asks.

"Yes, in fact, I do all the time. But only for two types of men: Jewish men and Native Americans."

"Why is that?" he asks.

"Because Jewish men are wonderful lovers," she says. "They are considerate, eager to please, and they don't have a lot of hangups. Native American men are passionate lovers. They've been treated very badly by this country, and they have a lot of anger. When they channel that anger into sexual passion, it's unbelievably good."

"That's really interesting," the man says. "Did I introduce myself? My name's Hyman Littlefoot."

• BAWDY •

A hooker, a man sitting next to her

The first-class section of an airplane

 A man adapts to a beautiful woman's taste.

The Nasty Parrot and
the One-Eyed Man

Another visual joke . . . follow the cue at the end.

A man walks into a pet store and spots the most beautiful parrot he's ever seen. Its feathers are more colorful than any other he has seen. Its beak is perfect, and the bird stands on its perch as if awaiting coronation. He has to have that parrot. He asks the owner how much he wants for it.

"I'm sorry," the owner says, "but I can't sell you that particular bird."

"Look," the man says, "if this is your way of negotiating a really high price, don't bother. I'm one of the richest men in town. I don't care what he costs. I'm not going to leave this store without that bird!"

"No, that's not it," the owner says. "The price would be cheap because there's a serious problem with that bird. It's *nasty,* that one is. It's profane, and it picks on people. For instance, and I mean no offense, but I notice that you wear an eye patch. That bird would only make fun of you."

The man looks at the store owner and says, "I think I can take abuse from a bird. How much?"

A deal is struck, and the man brings his parrot home. He's quite excited with his new purchase. He sets the new bird and its cage in a place of honor in his living room. He sets the parrot on the perch and says, "Polly want a cracker?"

The bird says, "Errrruh! Fuck you, you one-eyed bastard!"

Stunned, the man slaps the parrot, knocking it off its perch. The parrot gets up, dazed, and hops back on. Again, the man says, "Polly want a cracker?"

Much to the man's dismay, the bird says, "Errrruh! Fuck you, you one-eyed bastard!"

Not believing the insolence of this bird, the man throws it in the microwave and puts the microwave on high for 10 seconds. When he opens the door, the parrot is visibly shaken and staggers back to the perch. It takes the bird three tries on its wobbly legs to hop back on. Confident that the bird has learned the error of its ways, the man says, "*Now*, does Polly want a cracker?"

The bird, very slowly, says, "Errrruh! Fuck . . . you, . . . you . . . one-. . . eyed . . . bastard!"

Enraged, the man picks up the parrot, opens the freezer door, throws in the bird, and slams the door shut. Figuring to leave the bird in the freezer for 10 minutes—to really teach it a lesson—he sits down in front of a football game on television.

Three hours of football later, he realizes he's forgotten to let the parrot out. Knowing it must be dead, he opens the freezer door. Sure enough, the bird is frozen solid, like this:

(Facing the person you're telling the joke to, put your left hand over your left eye, and give them the finger with your right hand.)

· *G E N E R A L / B A W D Y* ·

 A one-eyed man, a parrot, a pet store owner

A pet shop, the one-eyed man's home

A parrot and owner clash. The parrot loses.

6 3

The Shipwrecked Man and the Woman in the Wet Suit

A shipwrecked man sits on the beach, idly looking out at the ocean, when he notices a dot approaching on the horizon. He squints and says to himself, "Hmm. Not big enough to be a ship." The dot gets closer, and he says, "That's not even a raft!"

Sure enough, the dot gets close enough for him to see that it's the top of a snorkel. Attached to that snorkel, a gorgeous blonde woman emerges from the water, wearing a tight wet suit. She walks right up to him and says, "Hey, fella, when was the last time you had a nice cigar?"

"Geez, it's been ten years," he says.

She unzips a little pocket on her wet suit, pulls out a watertight case, and from that case produces a Cuban cigar and a lighter. She lights the cigar and gives it to him.

Waving off his thanks, she says, "When was the last time you had a nice shot of whiskey?"

"Same as everything else, lady. It's been a decade."

She unzips another little pocket, pulls out a flask and a shot glass, and pours him a shot, which he drinks happily.

She smiles and says, "When was the last time you had some *real* fun?" as she starts to unzip the central zipper of her wet suit.

"Oh, my God," the man says. "Don't tell me you have golf clubs in there!"

• GENERAL •

 A shipwrecked man, a beautiful woman

A desert island

 A woman offers some of life's pleasures.

The Elephant and the Mouse

An elephant is walking through the brush one day when he hears a high-pitched squeak coming from a mouse trapped at the bottom of a shallow pit.

"Please help me," the trapped mouse cries. "You see, the walls of this pit are too slippery, and I cannot climb out."

"No problem," the elephant says, squatting down low enough to allow the mouse to use his penis like a ramp.

A month later, the mouse is walking through the brush when he hears a bugle-like call for help from the elephant trapped at the bottom of a huge pit.

"Please help me," the elephant cries. "You see, the walls of this pit are too slippery, and I cannot climb out."

"No problem," the mouse says, crouching as low as he can so the elephant can grab onto his penis and pull himself out. Realizing that this won't work, the mouse says, "Hold on, I'll be right back."

The mouse returns with his red Ferrari sports car. "Hook your trunk around the bumper," he tells the elephant. The elephant does so, and the mouse inches the car forward until the elephant is free.

The moral of the story: You don't need a large penis if you've got a red Ferrari.

• B A W D Y / G R O A N E R •

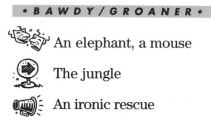

An elephant, a mouse

The jungle

An ironic rescue

The Hunchback's Replacement

After the Hunchback dies, Notre Dame needs a new bell-ringer. The head priest holds job interviews but cannot find anyone with the strength to ring the bell loud enough for all of Paris to hear.

One day, another hunchback comes looking for the position. The first thing the priest notices is that his arms hang down at his sides, useless.

In a raspy, slurred voice, the hunchback explains that he doesn't use his arms to ring the bell. To demonstrate, he runs across the platform and smashes his head into the bell, ringing it loudly.

The priest says, "That is very good, but perhaps not loud enough."

"May I try again?" the hunchback asks. "I can do better."

"By all means," says the priest.

With that, the hunchback runs across the platform again, ramming his head into the bell even harder, ringing it louder than before.

"I don't know," says the priest. "That was better, but I'm afraid it wasn't quite loud enough."

"Please," says the hunchback, "one more chance."

"Well, okay," says the priest.

This time, the hunchback finds the spot on the platform farthest from the bell and runs with all his might, launching himself at the bell. The sound his head makes is deafening. It is the loudest the bell has ever rung, and it draws a crowd. Unfortunately, the hunchback stumbles from his efforts and falls off the platform to his death.

Down in the square, the crowd looks at the lifeless body while the priest gives the hunchback last rites. A man asks the priest,

"Who was he?"

"I never got his name," says the priest, "but his face sure rings a bell."

. . . and a week later . . .

Another hunchback shows up at Notre Dame, looking to land the job that has still not been filled. He tells the priest he is the brother of the dead hunchback, and the priest brings him to the bell tower.

"Like my brother," rasps the hunchback, "I use my head to ring the bell."

And before the priest can warn him of the danger of falling, the hunchback runs at the bell, ringing it loudly with his head before losing his balance and falling to his death.

Another crowd gathers, and as the hunchback receives last rites, a man asks the priest, "Who was *he*?"

"Can't you tell?" asks the priest. "He's a dead ringer for his brother."

· GROANER ·

 A priest, two hunchbacks

 Notre Dame

Two hunchbacks use their noggins, and lose their lives.

The Golfer's Three Wishes

While a golfer is looking for his ball that he sliced into the woods, he comes upon an old lamp. Seeing an inscription on the side that's caked with dirt, he rubs it with his handkerchief. As soon as he does this, a genie appears.

"You have rescued me," the genie says. "I will grant you three wishes."

"Wow," says the golfer, "Okay, first . . ."

"WAIT!" the genie bellows. "First, I must ask, do you have a wife?"

"Yeah," the golfer says.

"Okay, then," the genie says. "Whatever things you wish for yourself, she will receive twice as much of."

"Fine," the guy says. "First of all, I want a handicap of zero."

"Your wish is granted. I've taken 12 strokes off your game, so you are at zero. I've also taken 24 strokes off your wife's game, so she's now at minus 4, which means she's a better golfer than you are."

The golfer isn't happy about this, but he presses on. "Okay, second, I want 20 million dollars in my bank account."

"Your wish is granted," says the genie. "I've put 20 million dollars into your private account. I've put 40 million in your wife's separate account, which means she's twice as wealthy as you are."

The golfer is now in a real funk. He thinks for a few minutes and says, "She gets twice what I get? Okay, I want to have a *mild* heart attack."

· G O L F / G E N I E ·

 A golfer, a genie

A golf course

A golfer's third wish is the charm.

6 8

The Reluctant Parachutist

A young soldier returns home on leave, and his father asks about training camp. "I have to tell you, Dad, it was the hardest time of my life. And *nothing* was scarier than the day they took us up in a plane and told us we had to parachute. You know how scared I am of heights."

The father says, "What did you do?"

"What did I do? Well, to be honest, I froze. I could not make my body jump out of that plane. Finally, my drill sergeant—the biggest, meanest man I have ever met—Comes right up to me and screams right in my ear, 'Son, you will jump off this plane! You will jump now! If you do not jump right now, I will take your sorry hide to the front of this plane and I will have my way with you!'"

The father asks, "Did you jump?"

The soldier says, "Oh yeah, Dad. But only a little."

• B A W D Y •

A young soldier, his father

The soldier's home

A soldier doesn't conquer his fear of heights.

The
Four Successful Sons

Four women are playing bridge when the conversation turns toward their children.

"My son is a brilliant accountant, one of the smartest in the country," says the first woman. "The best accountant in the city by far. He's so successful that last year he not only bought himself a Porsche, but he also bought one for a friend."

"Well, *my* son is a doctor," says the second woman. "The most respected doctor in the county. He's so successful that last year he not only bought himself a speedboat, but he also bought one for a friend."

"That's all very nice," says the third woman. "*My* son is a lawyer. The highest paid lawyer in the state. He bills more per hour than most people make in a week. He's so successful that last year he not only bought himself a mansion, but he also bought one for a friend."

The fourth woman says nothing, until the first woman asks, "What about your son?"

The fourth woman says, "He's a homosexual." The other women are shocked. Finally, the first woman says, "But what does he *do*?"

"Nothing," says the fourth woman. "He doesn't have to. Last year his boyfriends *gave* him a Porsche, a speedboat, and a mansion."

· G E N E R A L ·

Four women playing bridge

A bridge game

Bragging rights uncover a secret.

The Drinker's Pocket

A man walks into a bar and orders a shot of whiskey, neat. After drinking it in one gulp, he pulls open the breast pocket on his shirt and looks inside. After a moment he orders a second shot of whiskey, neat.

When he's finished drinking the second shot, he looks into his shirt pocket again, before deciding to order a third.

The bartender sees this, and after watching the man repeat the action through six shots of whiskey, the bartender says, "Sir, it's none of my business, but may I ask why you look into your pocket after every drink?"

"Sure," says the man. "In my pocket I keep a picture of my wife, and after every drink I look at it. When she starts to look good, I go home."

· **B A R R O O M** ·

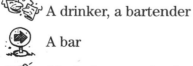 A drinker, a bartender

A bar

Alcohol cures a husband's reticence to go home.

The Bank President's Easy Bet

One Friday morning, a woman walks into the bank with a rather large briefcase and tells a bank officer that she'd like to open a new account. When the bank officer asks how much she'd like to deposit, she cooly responds, "One million dollars. In cash."

Amazed, the bank officer says, "Why that would be the largest personal deposit we've ever had. I'm sure that the president of the bank would like to see to your account personally," and he leads her to the president's office.

After her situation has been explained to him, the president asks, "Just out of curiosity, may I inquire how it is that you make your money?"

"Of course," the woman says. "I'm a gambler."

"Isn't that risky?" he asks.

"I only bet on sure things," she says.

"There's no such thing," he tells her.

"That's silly. Of course there is. And in fact, I'll make you a bet, if you'd like."

Saying that it is against the rules of the bank for him to gamble, he demurs. Still, he asks her what she would have bet on if he had decided to indulge her.

"Simple," she tells him. "I am prepared to bet you this one million dollars that by next Monday morning, your testicles will be square as cubes."

"That's impossible," he says. "In fact, that's so absurd that I'll break the rules and take you up on your bet. See you right here at ten o'clock on Monday morning."

That night, he reaches down and assures himself that his testicles are indeed still round. On Saturday morning, he does it again, just to be on the safe side, as he does three times on Saturday night and six times on Sunday. Every time, his testicles are just the same shape that they've always been.

On Monday morning, he checks one last time before going to work. Confident that he has won the ridiculous bet, he goes to the office.

At ten, the woman shows up with a large man carrying a suitcase. "I have terrible news for you," the bank president tells her. "I've just checked and it seems that you've lost. If you'd sign these papers, turning over your deposit to me, I'd appreciate it."

"For that kind of money," she asks, "would you mind if I verified this myself?"

"Be my guest," the bank president says. With that, she walks across the room, unbuttons the bank president's pants, and reaches inside. As she does this, the large man with the suitcase faints dead away.

"What's the matter with him?" the bank president asks.

"Well," the woman says, "on Friday I bet him *ten* million dollars that by Monday morning I'd have the president of the bank by the balls."

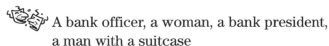

 A bank officer, a woman, a bank president, a man with a suitcase

The bank president's office

An outrageous bet pays off.

Naive Maria's Wedding Night

As young Maria goes upstairs in her parent's house, per tradition, to consummate her marriage, she's nervous. Her mother reassures her, "If you have any questions, I will be here stirring the soup."

Maria goes upstairs, and her husband starts undressing. Seeing hair on his chest, she runs downstairs to her mother. "Momma," she says, "he took off his shirt, ana he'sa got hair on his chest!"

Her mother says, "Maria, you have lived a very sheltered life. Most men, unlike you father ana you brother, have hair on their chest."

Back upstairs, Maria sees hair on his legs and again runs to her mother. "Momma," she says, "he took off his pants, ana he'sa got hair on his legs!"

Her mother says, "Maria, it'sa just like the hair on the chest. Justa because you father ana you brother don'a have hair on their legs, don'a think no one else does." Again, Maria goes back upstairs.

When she gets to the bedroom, her husband is naked, and she notices that the front of his right foot is gone. Seeing her confusion, he says, "It was blown off in the war." This is too much for Maria, who runs back to the kitchen. Looking up from the soup, her mother says, "Now what'sa the matta?"

Maria says, "He took off all his clothes, ana he'sa got a foot ana half!"

"A foot ana half?" her mother asks. "*You* stir the soup, *I'ma* go upstairs."

· B A W D Y ·

 Maria, her new husband, her mother

The kitchen

A daughter's panic results in a mother's awe.

The Golf Robots and the Union

The owner of a new golf course, eager to keep costs down, asks his club pro how he can find cheap labor to tend to the course.

"Easy," says the pro. "I have a friend who will build you a bunch of robots that can be programmed to groom the course round the clock. His prices are reasonable."

The owner goes to the friend and orders the robots. Two weeks later, he has 100 shiny metal robots working hard on his course. A week after that, the pro comes to him with bad news.

"The local labor union president was here yesterday, and he's pissed that you're not using union guys. He says he can make trouble for you."

"Did you tell him that I already paid for the robots?" asks the owner.

"Yeah, and he has a solution he says will make everybody happy. He'll rent you a hundred union uniforms at a dollar a week apiece, and he says that will keep the heat off you."

The owner shrugs and says, "What choice do I have? Go ahead and rent the uniforms."

That night, the pro puts the union uniforms on the robots.

The next day, only eight of the robots show up for work.

· G O L F ·

A golf course owner, a golf pro, 100 robots

A golf course

Robots quickly assimilate into the union.

Jesus at the Vatican

While wandering around St. Peter's Square in Vatican City, a priest spies Jesus over his shoulder, walking toward the Pope's office. Hurrying ahead of Jesus, the priest sees a bishop heading in the same direction and says to him, "The Pope must be warned at once that Jesus is on his way to see him!" The bishop agrees, and asks the priest to stall Jesus.

At the Pope's office, the bishop sees a cardinal just outside the office door. "Your Eminence," the bishop says, "Jesus is coming."

"That is what our faith tells us," the cardinal replies.

"No, he's coming now!" the bishop says. "Look over my shoulder!"

The cardinal immediately sees Jesus, who is fast approaching. "You stall him," the cardinal says, "while I warn the Pope."

Entering the Pope's office, the cardinal says, "Your Holiness, forgive the intrusion, but Jesus is walking this way even as we speak."

The Pope looks at the cardinal, then bolts out of his chair and runs to the closet, where he gets out a typewriter. He places the typewriter on his desk and goes back to the closet for paper.

The cardinal repeats, "Your Holiness, I said that Jesus is on his way *right now!*"

The Pope says, "I heard you the first time. Now for God's sake, will you try to look busy!"

• R E L I G I O N •

 A priest, Jesus, a bishop, a cardinal, the Pope

 The halls of the Vatican, the Pope's office

The Pope panics at the arrival of Jesus.

The Dummy and
the Puzzle

A young man who is constantly on the receiving end of cruel jokes about his lack of intelligence decides to prove to his friends that he isn't as dumb as they think. He goes to the store and buys a jigsaw puzzle, and as soon as he's finished, he calls his friends over to see what he's done.

"You guys are always saying how dumb I am," he says, and they nod agreement. "Well, feast your eyes on *this*," he says, unveiling the finished puzzle.

They look at the puzzle, and at him. "So?" one of them says.

"I did this in just over one day," he says proudly.

They start snickering. "One day?" another one says. "There're only eight pieces in this puzzle! It should have taken you about thirty seconds."

"You can't make fun of me this time," the man says. "See the box it came in? It says right here on the box, 'Two to Four Years.'"

· G R O A N E R ·

A dumb guy, his friends

The dumb guy's house

A dumb guy brags about his ability to do a puzzle quickly.

The Golfer's Wife
and Mistress

A man is watching a golf match on TV when his wife asks him, "Honey, if I die, would you let your mistress wear my jewelry?"

Annoyed, he replies, "C'mon, that's stupid, I'm not even going to dignify that with an answer. Leave me alone, I'm trying to watch the match."

Not satisfied with her husband's noncommittal response to the first question, a few minutes later, the wife asks, "Honey, if I die, would you let your mistress drive my Mercedes?"

"Where does this come from?" he asks. "You're really being nuts. I told you, I'm not going to answer that kind of question. It's foolish and serves no point. Now leave me alone. Watching golf is one of the few pleasures I have."

A few minutes later, the wife persists with the same silly line of questioning, this time asking, "Honey, if I die, would you let your mistress use my golf clubs?"

The husband turns and looks her right in the eye. "Are you crazy?" he asks. "She's a lefty!"

· G O L F ·

 A golfer, his wife

Their living room

 Admission of an affair with a southpaw

The Foo Bird

Three intrepid explorers try to climb the highest mountain in Nepal, having been warned of the terrible Foo bird, feared for its deadly droppings. Thinking that the Foo bird stories are legend, they trek up the slopes anyway.

On a ledge hundreds of feet in the air, they are attacked by the giant Foo bird, who pelts them with his droppings until they are all standing neck-high in Foo dung.

The first explorer says, "Besides the smell, this is not so bad," and tries to wriggle free. Just as he's about to step free of the pile of droppings, he loses his balance and falls to his death.

The second explorer starts to wriggle, careful not to move so much that he will meet the same fate. With half his body free, he reaches up and grabs a lip on the rock. Just as he's free, the rock lip crumbles and he falls to his death.

After a day of keeping perfectly still, the third explorer notices that the dung is drying up and breaking off by itself. When most of it has fallen off, he decides to pull one foot out. What he doesn't realize is that there is a small pile of dung under his feet that hasn't dried yet; he slips on it and falls to his death.

The moral of the story: If the Foo shits, wear it.

• G R O A N E R •

 Three intrepid explorers

 A mountainside

Explorers deal with crap.

The
Earless Interviewer

Three men are applying for the same job in a detective agency that only handles the very delicate matters of wealthy, refined clients. Nervously, they wait in the reception area until, one at a time, they are led into the office of the agency's president.

"Good morning," the president says to the first man applying for the job. "You did very well on the written test, but it's of considerable more importance to us to see how you are at observing things. Look at me very closely, take a moment to collect your thoughts, and tell me what you notice."

"You don't got no fuckin' ears," the man says immediately, and indeed, the president doesn't.

The president shakes his head. "I see you go straight for the obvious, and you are a crude man. Well, neither of those traits will do in an agency of this stature. Thank you for your time. Good day, sir."

With that, the first man leaves and the second man is shown in. The president says to him, "You are a marvelous physical specimen, and I'm sure our clients would be most pleased to have you around not only for detection but also for *pro*tection. Still, it's most important to us that you have a well-developed sense of observation. So, look at me very closely, take a moment to collect your thoughts, and tell me what you notice."

"Well, first off," the second man says, "I see you got no fuckin' ears."

"Oh, dear," says the president. "Just like the last man in this room, you are vulgar and have an overly keen grasp of the obvious.

Unfortunately, you are not right for this job. Thank you for your time. Good day, sir."

As the second man is leaving, he decides to help out the third man, who has not yet been shown in. "Be polite," he whispers in the third man's ear, "and when he asks you a question, don't go for the obvious stuff."

The third man is shown into the office, and the president says, "Well, it's been a disappointing day. The first candidate, who was the smartest I've seen, failed my test of observation. So did the second candidate, who was the most physically superior. If *you* pass the test, the job is yours. I'd like for you to look at me very closely, take a moment to collect your thoughts, and tell me what you notice."

The third man looks for a moment, and says, "I see that you wear contacts."

The president beams. "That's excellent! You took your time, and made an observation that was not obvious; you have the job if you want it. But tell me please, how did you deduce that I wear contacts?"

"Easy," says the third man. "Where the fuck would you rest your glasses?"

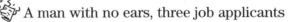
• G E N E R A L / B A W D Y •

 A man with no ears, three job applicants

The man's office

Three men fail a job test.

Paddy's Three Beers

Paddy walks into a bar and orders three beers. The bartender, noticing that he's alone, asks him why he wouldn't simply order one beer at a time like all of his other patrons at the bar.

"I'm from Ireland," Paddy says, "and me father and me uncle are still there, and I miss them somethin' fierce. So I order a round in their honor, and I drink the beers meself." Moved by this, the bartender buys the round for Paddy and leaves him alone to drink his beers in peace.

Every week for months, the same thing happens. Paddy comes in, says hello to the bartender, and orders his round of three beers—until one day, when he comes in, says hello to the bartender, and orders just two beers. Worried that something is amiss, the bartender says, "Paddy, I noticed you only ordered two beers. Is everything okay? Are your father and your uncle all right? You've been ordering three beers for months now. Why the change?"

Sipping one of the beers, Paddy says, "Oh, you're kind to ask, but me father and me uncle are fine. It's just that I've given up beer for Lent."

• BARROOM •

 Paddy, a bartender

 A bar

Consuming beer for relatives in abstentia

The Scientist and the Fokkers

A noted German scientist is asked to speak at the graduation ceremony of an all-girls high school. The principal asks the scientist to talk about his daring escape from Nazi Germany during World War II. Up at the podium, the scientist begins to tell his story:

"I vas vorking in ze lab vun day, und I vas looking at ze airfield nearby ven I saw a young pilot leaf his plane unattended vor chust vun minute. I saw mine chance, and stole ze plane. Chust as I'm leaving German airspace, close to freedom, I see three fokkers on mine tail . . ."

The principal interrupts, saying to the girls, "Fokkers, of course, were a type of German airplane."

The scientist, clearly annoyed at the interruption and seeking further clarification, says, "Yah, I know dat. But zese fokkers ver flying Messerschmidts!"

· G E N E R A L ·

 A German scientist, a school principal

A high-school graduation ceremony

Recounting a colorful wartime escape story

The Messenger's
Three Tests

A medieval messenger arrives at the castle of King Leo with terrible news for the king. Knowing that the king has a habit of killing any messenger that brings him news he doesn't like, the messenger says, "Your Highness, I have terrible news. But before I give it to you, I'd like to say that I don't think it's fair to kill a man for giving you bad news . . . after all, the news is not his fault."

"I agree with you," the king says, "now get on with it. Have my men lost a battle somewhere? Are there a few casualties? Tell me at once!"

"I'm afraid it's worse, sire," the messenger says. "It seems that your only son has died in battle."

The king rages. "Never mind what I said! You must pay for this news with your life!"

The messenger pleads, "But sire, surely there is some way you can spare my life."

After thinking a while, the king responds, "All right, I'll give you a chance to save your own life. I will give you three tests. Do you see those tents in the courtyard? Inside each tent is a test. In the first tent, there is a jug of wine. You must drink the wine in under one minute, and then emerge from the tent with the bottle upside down to show that it is empty. If you try to cheat, or if you don't come out within a minute, I'll have you killed."

"Yes, Your Highness," the messenger says, "and what are the other tests?"

"In the second tent," the king continues, "is a saber-toothed tiger with an impacted wisdom tooth, who hasn't eaten in a week. You must pull the tooth with your bare hands. When you emerge from the tent with the tooth, you can take the third test. In the third tent you will find the most beautiful maiden in the land, who is also the biggest nymphomaniac. She has never been satisfied by any man. *You* must satisfy her. When she emerges from the tent and declares herself completely satisfied, you will have completed the third test and I shall let you live."

On the king's command, the messenger dashes off to the first tent. He staggers out 55 seconds later, holding the empty wine bottle upside down. The king says, "You may now go on to the second test."

With that, the messenger staggers drunkenly into the second tent. Roars and screams come from the tent, and the king's court is sure that the messenger has been ripped apart by the tiger. Some minutes later, the tiger's roar subsides into panting. Then, to the astonishment of the entire court, the messenger staggers out of the tent, out of breath. "Okay," he says drunkenly, "where's the babe with the tooth problem?"

• *G E N E R A L / B A W D Y* •

 A king, a messenger

The king's castle

 A messenger "screws" up his test.

The Golfer, His Wife, and the Leprechaun's Wish

A man and his wife are golfing when the man slices a shot into the woods. Poking around in the brush with his club, he accidentally wakes a little man who is sleeping under a pile of leaves. "Son," the little man exclaims, "don't you know what you've done? You've woke the leprechaun!"

"I'm sorry," the man says. "Am I in some kind of trouble?"

"No, son," the leprechaun tells him. "When you wake the leprechaun, you get three wishes. Tell me, then. There must be something that you want."

The man thinks for a moment. "The only thing I ever really wanted was to be a scratch golfer."

"Done," the leprechaun says. "Tomorrow morning, you'll wake up and play the best game of your life. And from then on, you'll shoot par if not better on every course you play."

"Thank you so much," the man says.

"'Tis nothin'," the leprechaun says, "and you've still got two wishes."

"Well," the man says, "there *is* this mansion near the first tee that I've always wanted."

"Done," the leprechaun says. "Tomorrow morning, you'll wake up and find the deed to the mansion on your dresser. When you move in, you'll find all new, lovely furnishings."

"This is *great!*" the man says. "What more could I want?"

"Think," comes the reply, "surely there must be something . . ."

"Okay," the man says, "I guess I could use a million dollars to go with my new lifestyle."

"Done," the leprechaun says. "Tomorrow morning, you'll wake up and find a million dollars more in your bank account than you have today."

"This is too much," the man says. "Surely there's something I can do for you."

"Oh, no, son, but thanks . . ."

"Really, there must be something you want."

The leprechaun thinks for a moment, and says, "Well . . ."

"Anything," the man says. "Name it."

"I hate to ask," the leprechaun says, "but I noticed that you have a lovely wife there on the fairway. And you see, I've been alone for so long. I was wondering if I could maybe take a tumble with her?"

"Gee, I don't know," the man says. "She is my wife, and I don't know if she'd . . ." He stops, noticing the downcast look on the leprechaun's face. "Hey, you've been so nice, I could at least ask."

With that, the man goes out to talk to his wife. After explaining to her about his new golf abilities, the mansion, and the money, she agrees to the leprechaun's request. She goes into the woods and has sex with the leprechaun. Afterward, he says, "Lass, that was great. But may I ask you a question?"

"Sure," she says.

"How old is your husband, lass?"

"He's 35. Why do you ask?"

The leprechaun raises an eyebrow and says, "Don't you think 35 is a bit old to be believin' in leprechauns?"

• G O L F / B A W D Y •

 A golfer, his wife, a leprechaun

 In the woods by a golf course

Three futile wishes bless the giver.

The Tate Compass

Pierre, the world-famous explorer, is approached by the Tate Company to endorse their new line of compasses, and agrees.

The Tate Company promotional department comes up with an unheard-of publicity stunt: With Pierre's consent, the company arranges to have him blindfolded and led by other world-famous explorers into the heart of the jungle. Left there alone, with nothing but a few days' worth of food and water (and his brand new Tate's compass), he is to find his way back to civilization. The stunt is set to be the basis of the next Tate compass advertising campaign.

Something goes wrong, and Pierre does not return for many days. Finally, a rescue team is sent into the jungle to find him, much to the embarrassment of the Tate Company. They search and search but cannot find him.

Some months later, a safari group discovers Pierre's dead body. In one hand, he is clutching his compass, and in the other hand, he is clutching his notebook. On the last page of the notebook, they read these words: "It was the compass. It never worked. It led me in circles until my food and water ran out, and I'm afraid it has killed me."

Which is why, to this day, every good explorer knows this: He who has a Tate's is lost.

• G R O A N E R •

 Pierre the explorer

 The jungle

Pierre is killed by a faulty compass.

Jesus Tries to Prevent a Stoning

Jesus wanders into a small village and notices a commotion in the village square. He finds the villagers all gathered into an unruly mob, preparing to stone a woman to death for prostitution. Watching the scene escalate, Jesus feels bound to intervene and stop the stoning. Stepping to the front of the crowd, he says, "Let the one among you who is without sin cast the first stone."

A woman walks to the front of the crowd, picks up a rock, and BAM!, smashes the prostitute in the head. The prostitute falls to the ground, and Jesus shakes his head sadly. With that, the crowd whips itself into a full rock-throwing frenzy, finishing the job off.

Jesus grabs the woman by the arm, leads her away from the crowd, turns to her and says, "Mom, sometimes you really piss me off."

• R E L I G I O N •

Jesus, the first rock-thrower

 A New Testament village

 The Virgin Mary sullies her reputation.

The Diagnostic 2000

Worried about the pain in his arm, a man goes to see his doctor. When the doctor asks for a urine sample, he is confused.

"Come into the examination room and let me show you our new machine," the doctor says, leading the way.

Once inside the room, the doctor takes the urine sample and pours it into a tube leading to a large machine. After some whirring noises, a piece of paper comes out the other end. "Our new Diagnostic 2000 says that you have tennis elbow," the doctor says.

The man laughs. "Your machine stinks; I don't play tennis."

The doctor says, "This machine is never wrong. Tennis elbow it is."

Ticked off, the man leaves. The next day, still angry about the doctor's diagnosis, he gets an idea. He takes a jar and collects some of his wife's urine and his car engine's oil, and for good measure, he masturbates into it.

Back at the doctor's office, he says that he's not feeling well and produces the jar as his urine sample. The doctor feeds it into the machine, which starts to sputter and cough, and a piece of paper comes out the other end. The doctor studies it for a moment and says, "Your wife is pregnant by the milkman, your car needs a tune-up, and now I know why you have tennis elbow."

 A doctor, his patient

The doctor's office

Attempting to fool a sophisticated piece of equipment

The Foul-Mouthed
Bank Customer

A man walks into a bank, and after waiting for 20 minutes in line, he goes straight to a customer service representative and says, "Hey, lady, I got this here check for deposit, and I'll be goddamned if I'm gonna wait my ass on line anymore."

"Please," says the woman. "I won't have that kind of language in this bank."

"Well, excuse me, but this fuckin' check ain't drawing any goddamned interest with you yappin' away about my language."

"Sir," she says, "I don't have to take this abuse . . ."

"Well then let's get the fuckin' manager, okay? I mean, what kind of shit is this I have to take from you?"

The manager is summoned, and says, "What seems to be the problem?"

The woman says, "This man is using vulgar language and I won't stand for it."

The man says, "Hey, alls I'm trying to do in this goddamned bank, for Christ's sake, is deposit this fuckin' check for 15 million dollars."

The manager looks at the check, then at the man, and says, "And this fuckin' bitch won't help you?"

• BAWDY •

 A foul-mouthed man, a customer service representative, a bank manager

A bank

An unruly customer becomes a "friend" of the bank.

The Snakebitten Golfer

A man and his friend are out playing golf when the man slices his ball into the woods. After fifteen minutes of digging through the brush with his golf club, looking for the ball, he accidentally hits a rattlesnake, who immediately jumps up and bites him through the front of his pants. His friend, hearing his howls of pain, rushes into the woods and finds him on the ground, writhing around in the leaves, holding his crotch, and moaning in obvious and extreme agony.

"What happened?" the friend asks.

"HE BIT ME!" the man screams. "PLEASE, YOU HAVE TO DO SOMETHING . . . IT HURTS!"

"Let me see," the friend says. After helping the man pull his pants down, he sees that the snake has bitten the man right on the tip of his penis. "Look, I'm not a doctor, but I know that you have to keep still to slow the spread of the venom," he tells his friend, who is panicking. "Wait here while I drive the golf cart back to the clubhouse. I'll call a doctor and ask him what to do. I'll be back as soon as I can."

"Okay," the man says, a little calmer. "But HURRY!"

Once he's gotten back to the clubhouse, the friend phones the doctor. "Doc," he says, "my golf partner's been bitten by a rattlesnake. He's lying in the woods and I'm afraid to move him. I told him to lie still while I call you. He's in an awful lot of pain, Doc. What can I do?"

"Can you find the puncture wounds?" the doctor asks.

"Yes."

"Good. Now listen carefully. Take a sharp knife—make sure you get it as clean as possible—and cut an X in the flesh right where the bite marks are."

"But that's going to hurt," the man protests.

"If you don't, he'll die. Next, put your mouth over the X, and suck all the poison out. Be sure not to swallow any. After that, bandage the wound as best you can, call an ambulance, and bring him right to me."

"Geez, Doc. Do I have to do this?"

"Like I said, if you don't, your golf partner is going to die."

"Got it. Thanks, Doc." With that, the man hangs up the phone and races out of the clubhouse, jumps in the golf cart, and drives to the spot in the woods where his friend is lying, now in a state of complete hysteria.

"Did you talk to the doctor?" the stricken man asks.

"Yes, I did."

"Well? What did he say?"

"He said you're gonna die."

• G O L F / B A W D Y •

 Two golfers, a doctor

 In the woods by a golf course

 Golf partners test their friendship over a snakebite.

The Hippies and the Dangerous Turn

On a hippy commune located on California's Pacific coastline, a new road is built. There is a particularly hairy left turn on the road, and six of the first ten people who attempt to make the turn in their cars skid over the edge and plunge off a cliff to their death.

The four who made the turn with no problem are sitting around, talking about their luck.

"I can't believe it," says the first hippy, "'cause I had made that turn after smoking three joints."

"You, too?" asks the second. "I made that turn after taking a few hits off a bong filled with killer weed."

"That's odd," says the third, "I was smoking dope all day before making that turn."

"Me, too," says the fourth. "And now that I think of it, none of the autopsies of the guys who didn't make the turn showed any drugs in their system. They were all straight."

The hippies talk a little while longer, and decide what they must do. The next day, they erect a new traffic sign near the scene of the fatal accidents: NO LEFT TURN UNSTONED.

• G R O A N E R •

 Assorted stoned hippies

 A hippy commune

Four hippies solve a mystery.

The World Leaders and the Parachute

Three world leaders—an American president, a Russian president, and a Third World dictator—are the only passengers on an airplane. They are informed by the pilot that the plane is going to crash, and that there is only one parachute. The three argue over who should use it.

The American says, "As the leader of the free world, I am the most important man here. I should get the parachute."

The Russian says, "As the leader of the largest nation on earth, I am the most important man here. *I* should get the parachute."

The dictator says, "Gentleman, please. The only fair way to settle this is for the three of us to vote."

The other two agree, and as they do, the dictator puts the chute on and says, "I win, 10 to 2!"

• GENERAL •

 An American president, a Russian president, a dictator

A doomed airplane

 Fighting over the single parachute

The Third Grade Morals Lesson

Miss Jones is teaching her little third graders about stories with morals. At the end of the lesson, she asks her students if they know any stories with morals that they could share with the class.

Susie raises her hand and is called on. "Well," she says, "when my mommy was a little girl, her job was to go to the store on her bicycle and get the eggs. Her bike had two baskets in the back, one on the left and one on the right. One day, she put all the eggs on the right side, and the bike was unbalanced. It fell over, and all the eggs broke."

"And what's the moral?" asks Miss Jones.

"Don't put all your eggs in one basket," says Susie.

"Very good. Anyone else?"

Tommy raises his hand and is called on. "Well," he says, "when my daddy was a little boy, it was his job to count all the chickens every day at noon. One day, he wanted to leave early to play with his friends, so he counted all the chickens at nine o'clock, plus a few eggs that he thought would hatch by noon. When they didn't hatch, and his daddy found out what he did, countin' the chickens early and going out to play, he got a whuppin'."

"And what's the moral?" asks Miss Jones.

"Don't count your chickens before they're hatched," says Tommy.

"Excellent. One more?"

Little Eddie raises his hand and says, "I got one."

Miss Jones looks around the room, desperately, but no one else is raising a hand.

"C'mon, Teach," Eddie says. "I said I got one."

"Very well, Eddie, what is it?"

"My old man was a paratrooper in doubleya doubleya two, and before every mission he and his buddies would down a bottle of Jack Daniels. One day, before a particularly dangerous mission behind German lines, they each had their own bottle of J.D. They jump out of the plane, drunk out of their minds, and where does my old man land? Pow! Smack dab inna middle of 20 German bastards.

"He checks his gun, and he's only got two clips, nine bullets each. Eh-eh-eh-eh-eh-eh, he takes out 18 of those bastards. He sticks the bayonet into the gun, runs at one of the two still standing, and sticks the knife in the guy's ribs. He pushes that knife up and into that bastard's heart and kills him."

"Is that it?" asks Miss Jones, visibly shaken.

"Almost," says Eddie. "He grabs that last Nazi bastard by the face, spits on him, smashes his head into a rock, and strangles him. That's it."

"What on earth is the moral?" asks Miss Jones.

"Oh, that's easy," says Eddie. "Don't fuck with the old man when he's been drinkin'."

· C L A S S R O O M ·

 Miss Jones, Susie, Tommy, Little Eddie

 A classroom

A story is told with a "Little Eddie" moral.

Paddy's Last Day

It's the last day of Paddy's 40-year career delivering mail in his little Irish village. When he arrives at the home of the very mean town constable, the constable's gorgeous young wife invites Paddy in for breakfast. After explaining that the constable has gone to work, she lays out the most incredible breakfast spread Paddy's ever seen: pancakes, sausages, eggs cooked in all varieties, a big, juicy steak . . . needless to say, Paddy takes his time, and eats until he's stuffed.

As he's wiping his mouth, the constable's wife reappears in the kitchen, wearing only a flimsy negligee, and says, "Paddy, would you like to come upstairs with me, then?"

Paddy's eyes bulge out of his head, and he says, "I'd *love* to, ma'am, but I'm a wee bit afraid of the constable."

"Don't worry, Paddy," she tells him. "It's okay. Come on, then."

They go upstairs, and have incredible sex. After Paddy has dressed and is heading downstairs, the constable's wife hands him a pound note. Paddy says, "What's this for, lass?"

The constable's wife says, "When I asked me husband what I should give you for your retirement, he said, 'Give 'im a pound note and fuck 'im.' Breakfast was my idea."

· **B A W D Y** ·

 Paddy, the constable's wife

 The constable's house

Paddy receives a special retirement gift.

Tommy's Anatomy Lesson

L ittle Tommy happens to walk into his parents' room while his father is changing. He is obviously very confused at what he sees. Pointing at his father's privates, he asks, "Dad, what's that?"

Not embarrassed in the slightest by his son's curiosity, Tommy's father replies proudly, "Well, son, that's my penis. In fact, it's the perfect penis."

"Oh," Tommy says as he wanders out of the room, clearly in deep thought about what he saw.

The next day, while walking to school with little Susie, Tommy says, "Come here, into the bushes. I want to show you something." Once in the bushes, he pulls his pants down and points to his penis.

"What's that?" Susie asks.

"That's my penis," he says. "In fact, if it were two inches shorter, it would be the perfect penis."

· BAWDY ·

Tommy, his father, Susie

The father's bedroom, the bushes on the way to school

Tommy shows Susie his penis.

9 9

The
Vicious Attack
Bird

A man walks into a pet store and notices a particularly beautiful little bird in a cage. He is mesmerized by the little bird and amazed that he's never seen one like it before. He decides that he must have it. He asks the store owner, "How much is this bird?"

"Oh, I can't sell you that one. Sorry," says the owner. "Is there anything else I can show you today?"

"Why can't I buy that one?"

"He's too dangerous," says the owner.

The man can't believe it. "This pretty little bird? No way. What kind of bird is he?"

"This," the owner says, taking the little bird from the cage on his finger, "is a Vicious Attack Bird."

"You must be joking," says the man as he examines the tiny, delicate bird up close.

"I assure you I'm not," says the owner. "Would you like a demonstration?" The man nods, and the owner says, "Watch this." And to the bird he says, "Vicious Attack Bird: Pencil."

With that, the Vicious Attack Bird reaches into the owner's shirt pocket with its beak and pulls out his pencil. In a few violent seconds, it has pecked the pencil into nothing more than shavings. The demonstration complete, the bird returns to the store owner's finger.

"Impressive," says the man.

"You think that's impressive?" asks the owner. "Watch this." And to the bird he says, "Vicious Attack Bird: Chair."

With that, the Vicious Attack Bird leaps off the owner's finger and flies across the room to a chair that, thankfully, no one is sitting in. Within one minute, the bird has torn all the stuffing from the cushioning and reduced the chair legs to sawdust. All that remains intact are the metal coils in the seat cushion. Afterward, the bird calmly returns to its perch on the owner's finger.

"That's amazing," says the man. "I have to have it. Price is absolutely no object. Please. I will treat this remarkable animal with nothing but respect."

"Well . . ." says the owner, "as long as you're aware of the very real danger, and you're extremely careful with him, I don't see why you shouldn't have him."

The man pays for the bird and leaves the store with it perched on his shoulder. As he's walking down the street, a huge man steps in his path. "What are you, a sissy?" the huge man says. "What kind of wimpy bird is that?"

"This, my good man, is a Vicious Attack Bird."

The huge man scoffs and says, "Vicious Attack Bird, my ass."

· G E N E R A L ·

A pet store owner, a customer, a bully

A pet store, the street

A bird's particular talent teaches a bully a lesson.

The Frog's Collateral

A frog goes into a bank and asks about securing a small loan. After waiting for a while, he is shown to the office of Patricia Whack, the bank loan officer.

"I'm Patty," she says, by way of introduction. "How can I help you?"

"I'd like a loan so that I can fix up my lily pad," the frog says.

"I see on your application that you don't need much money," she says, "but I'll still need some collateral."

"No problem," says the frog, who pulls a small object out of a paper bag. He hands it to Patty and says, "It's been in my family for generations."

Patty looks closely at the object but has no idea what it is. "This is nice," she says, "but what does it do?"

"Nothing," says the frog. "It just sits on an end table. Isn't it beautiful?"

"Yes," she says. "Excuse me a moment." With that, Patty goes to the office of the bank manager, and says, "I have a frog out there who wants a small loan, and this is what he gave me as collateral. I'm sorry to bother you, but I have no idea how to describe this . . . can you tell me how to classify it?"

The bank manager, annoyed at the intrusion, looks the object up and down and says, "It's a knickknack, Patty Whack. Give the frog a loan."

· G R O A N E R ·

 A frog, Patricia Wack, a bank manager

 A bank

 An unrecognizable object is offered as collateral.

Frank Perdue and the Pope

Chicken magnate Frank Perdue goes to Rome to meet with the Pope. "Holy Father," he says, "I have a proposition for you. If you will change one word in one prayer, I will donate $25 million to the church, which you can use any way you like."

The Pope says, "Mr. Perdue, prayers are not for sale. But out of curiosity, what exactly is the change you'd like?"

"In the Our Father," Perdue explains, "I'd like you to change 'our daily bread' to 'our daily chicken'—and I'll up my offer to $50 million."

"I'm sorry," the Pope says, "but it wouldn't be right."

"Look," Perdue says, "you're obviously a tough negotiator, so I'll get to my final offer. Your Holiness, I am prepared to give the church $100 million dollars in return for this one change. Think of the good that money would do!"

The Pope thinks for a minute and says, "Very well. I will go tell the College of Cardinals about our deal."

The next day, the Pope speaks to the cardinals. "My brothers," he says, "I have some good news and some bad news. The good news is that we have gained $100 million for our charities throughout the world. The bad news is we lost the Wonder account."

• R E L I G I O N •

Frank Perdue, the Pope

 The Vatican

 Perdue negotiates with the Pope.

The Pianist and
the Peeing Monkey

A man walks into a bar and sits down near the piano, where he notices a performing monkey doing a cute little dance while the pianist plays. When the monkey gets close enough, the man pets him, which causes the monkey to pee in his drink. The man is slightly taken aback, and worried that he may have encouraged the monkey to urinate by petting him.

Feeling that maybe he shouldn't touch the monkey, the man asks the bartender for a new drink. As soon as he gets it, the monkey walks over and pees in it. The man is now completely confused and beginning to get a little angry with the monkey.

Rather than cause a scene, the man goes to a booth on the other side of the bar, and orders yet another new drink. As it's served, the monkey dances across the bar, jumps to the floor, climbs up into the booth, and pees in the drink. The man is now incensed and starting to believe that someone might be playing a sick joke on him.

The man goes over to the piano player and says, "Do you know your monkey keeps peeing in my drink?"

"No," the pianist says, "but maybe if you hum a few bars I'll remember it."

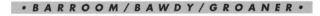

A man, a monkey, a pianist

A bar

 A monkey keeps peeing in drinks.

Naughty Dogs
Compare Stories

Two dogs, a little dog and a big dog, are in the waiting room at the vet's office. They've been waiting for a while, and to kill some time the big dog says to the little dog, "What are you in for?"

The little dog says, "I've been peeing on my owner's carpet, and she's pretty angry with me. I've done it for nearly two weeks straight now. I just can't stop. She says if the doctor can't figure out how to stop me from doing it, she's gonna have me put to sleep. What are *you* in for?"

The big dog says, "Every night for the past week, when my owner comes home, I've been running up to her in the hall, pushing her down, tearing her clothes off with my teeth, and having really wild sex with her."

"Oh, my," says the little dog. "Is the doctor going to put you to sleep?"

"No," says the big dog. "My owner's having my nails clipped and seeing about doggie breath spray."

· BAWDY ·

 A little dog, a big dog

 The waiting room at the veterinarian's

Two dogs compare very different fates.

The Blind Bunny and the Blind Snake

A blind bunny accidentally hops into a blind snake one day. "Excuse me," says the bunny, "but I'm blind and cannot see."

The snake says, "What a coincidence! I can't see either. What kind of animal are you?"

The bunny thinks for a moment and says, "You know, I've never really been sure . . . perhaps you can help me figure it out."

The snake coils itself around the bunny, feeling its features. When it's done, it says, "You have long, floppy ears, whiskers around your nose, and a cottony tail. You must be a bunny rabbit."

The bunny thanks the snake and asks, "What kind of animal are you?"

The snake thinks for a minute and says, "You know, I've never really been sure . . . perhaps *you* could help *me* figure it out."

The rabbit feels around the snake for a moment, and when it's done, it says, "You're slimy, you have beady eyes, you slither, and you have no balls. You must be an attorney."

• *L A W Y E R* •

A rabbit, a snake

The forest

 A bunny find similarities between snakes and lawyers.

The Nazi Clock
Torture

In a German POW camp during World War II, Commandant Fritz is using various psychological tortures on the prisoners to break their spirit over time. One day, he comes up with a task so boring, so repetitive, that he knows he will drive them absolutely crazy in a very short amount of time.

"Men," he tells the assembled prisoners, "today you vill stand zere perfectly still and you vill keep time for me. You vill tilt your head to ze left and say 'Tic' and zen to ze right and say 'Toc.' You vill do zis until I tell you to stop!"

Walking among the rows, he notices that all the men are doing as he says, tilting their heads left while saying "Tic," and then to the right while saying "Toc." He continues to wander through their ranks, very amused and impressed with himself for devising such a fiendishly stupid, yet wonderfully effective, torture. All the men are following his orders except for one: Colonel Smith, who is only tilting his head to the left, over and over, saying "Tic" each time.

"Vell, Colonel Smith," Fritz says to him, "you are a brave and defiant man. But as you know, ve have vays of making you 'Toc.'"

• G R O A N E R •

 Fritz the Nazi, Colonel Smith

A German POW camp

A Nazi taunts his prisoners.

The Slow Golfers

A foursome goes out on the course, only to find themselves waiting on every hole for the most inept golfers they've ever seen, who are playing in front of them. After a few holes, they start yelling at the klutzes, but that doesn't seem to speed their play. By the time they've finished their round, they're so pissed off that they go straight to the golf pro to complain.

"Guys," he tells them, "those fellas you've been screaming at and taunting for the last three hours are *blind*."

"You're telling us," one of the irate foursome says.

"No, I mean it," the pro says, "they're really blind. They're trying to overcome their handicap by participating in sports."

Now embarrassed, the first of the foursome says to the pro, "When they come in, fix 'em up with new golf shoes, and put it on my tab. Tell 'em we're sorry."

The second guy adds, "And while you're at it, give 'em each a new set of club covers, and put it on my tab."

The third one chimes in, "Listen, let 'em each pick out a new golf shirt, and put that on *my* tab."

They all stand there, waiting for the fourth guy to contribute something. Noticing their stares, he says, "What? Fuck 'em. Let 'em play at night."

· G O L F ·

 A foursome of golfers, a golf pro

 A golf course, the pro shop

Three of four golfers express remorse for rushing blind golfers.

Little Joey's Prayer

Little Joey is growing up in the projects, wishing he had a bicycle. His mother, who is broke and without a husband, gives him a plastic statue of the Virgin Mary to put on top of his dresser and tells him that if he wants a bike, he must ask the Virgin Mary every night in his prayers.

That night, at the end of his usual prayers, he says, ". . . and I'd like to make a special prayer to you, Virgin Mary. I've been a good boy, and I'd like a bike. Nothing fancy, just a 5-speed. Amen."

Joey does this every night for a month, and nothing happens. His mother tells him he must not be asking in the right way. So that night, at the end of his usual prayers, he says, ". . . and I'd like to make a special prayer to you, Virgin Mary. I've been very good, but I'd be even better if I had a 5-speed bike. Amen."

Another month goes by, and still nothing happens. His mother tells him once again that he must not be asking in the right way. So that night, little Joey takes the statue of the Virgin Mary off of his dresser and puts it in a sock. He wraps the sock in a T-shirt and puts the T-shirt in a shoe box, which he hides under the dresser. Then, after saying his usual prayers, he says, ". . . and I'd like to make a special prayer to you, Jesus. I want a bike, and if you ever want to see your mother again . . ."

• R E L I G I O N •

Little Joey, his mother

Joey's bedroom

Joey blackmails Jesus.

Third Grade Bedtime Rituals

Miss Jones is lecturing on the importance of family traditions and asks her students to give examples of bedtime rituals in their homes.

"In my house," says Tommy, "we all watch television until nine o'clock, and my mommy and daddy tell us a story sometimes, then tuck us in."

"Very good," says Miss Jones. "Anyone else?"

"In my house," says Susie, "we all have a small snack just before bed, and Daddy reads us a story."

"That's another good example," says Miss Jones. "Anyone else want to share?"

Little Eddie says, "In my house, I watch television alone while my daddy tries to keep my mommy from going to see the Lord."

Miss Jones feels terrible. "I didn't know your mother was sick, Eddie."

"She's not," he says. "But when I peek in their bedroom every night, Daddy is lying on top of Mommy, holding her to the bed, and her arms and legs are pointing up at heaven while she's screaming, 'Oh, God, I'm coming!'"

• CLASSROOM / BAWDY •

 Miss Jones, Tommy, Susie, Little Eddie

 A classroom

Little Eddie describes his parents' sexual habits.

The
Indecent Question

A man and a woman are chatting at a cocktail party. Changing the subject abruptly, the man asks, "Would you sleep with a strange man for $100?"

The woman looks offended and says, "I most certainly would not."

"Would you sleep with a strange man for $1,000?" he asks.

The woman says, "I most certainly would not."

"Would you sleep with a strange man for $10,000?" he asks.

The woman says, "I still wouldn't do it."

"Would you sleep with a strange man for $100,000?"

She thinks for a moment and says, "No, I wouldn't."

"Okay," says the man. "Would you sleep with a strange man for $1,000,000?"

"Yes," the woman says. "I would sleep with a strange man for $1,000,000."

"So," says the man, "you're a prostitute."

The woman is mortified. "You think I'm a prostitute?"

"Well, we've just established that you are," says the man. "Now we're just haggling over price."

 • *BAWDY* •

 A man, a woman

 A cocktail party

A wise guy tricks a woman.

The Princess and the Bushman

A bored, spoiled princess from Long Island decides to go on safari for a few weeks. While walking through the jungle, she gets confused and is separated from her safari guide and is lost.

Wandering aimlessly, she is discovered by a bushman, who takes her forcibly into his hut and has his way with her. For three days, he does nothing but violate her, in every position imaginable . . . in every orifice imaginable. Finally, he leaves the hut out of hunger. While he is hunting, a rescue party finds her and brings her safely back to civilization.

For weeks, she sits in her home on Long Island, somber and motionless. Her body is recovered, but she barely eats or talks. She just sits there.

Finally, a few months later, her sister confronts her. "You've been moping around here for a long time," the sister says. "I know you went through a terrifying ordeal, but you're safe now. You seem to be in good physical shape . . . so what's the matter?"

The woman sighs and stares out the window as she says, "He doesn't call, he doesn't write . . ."

· BAWDY ·

 A spoiled Long Island princess, her sister, a bushman

The jungle, a luxury home

 A spoiled woman misses the unexpected "romance" of her trip.

The Pilfered Rone

Buck and Trapper, two Canadian hunters, have a bet about who can catch more moose over one weekend during hunting season. Buck, anxious to win, studies moose intently for months leading up to the season and invents a moose mating call device he dubs a "rone."

Trapper does nothing to prepare, and on the first day of their contest he notices that Buck is having greater success with his rone than Trapper is having sitting quietly and waiting for the moose to wander into his sights without any encouragement.

That night, Trapper sneaks into Buck's tent while Buck is asleep and takes the rone, sure that he'll be able to easily win the contest with it.

On Sunday, Trapper blows the rone constantly, but with no results. At the end of the day, he concedes victory to Buck and admits his crime. Buck explains that a rone has to be calibrated to each man's blowing ability so that the sound is just right; otherwise, the noise is useless.

Or, in other words: A stolen rone gathers no moose.

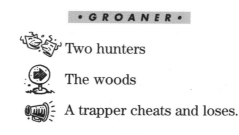

• G R O A N E R •

Two hunters

The woods

A trapper cheats and loses.

The Lawyer and the
Wind Currents

Two men strike up a conversation outside a packed New York City convention hall filled with lawyers.

"These Bar Association meetings are so dull I could scream," says one exasperated man, introducing himself as a local news legal reporter.

"They sure are," says the other man, a lawyer. "Say, you live in this city. Is there anything interesting to do to kill some time between conferences?"

"Sure," says the reporter. "In fact, come with me and I'll show you one of the most amazing natural phenomena in the world. Very few people know about it, and it occurs right across the street at the Empire State Building."

Curious, the lawyer agrees to go, and they head to the top of the Empire State Building.

"Watch this," the reporter says, jumping over the railing. The lawyer is horrified, thinking that the reporter is falling to his death. But then, as the reporter is halfway down the side of the building, his fall stops, and he begins to circle the building, as if being tossed by the wind. After three complete circles, he rises back up and slowly floats down to land on the exact spot he leaped from with not so much as a hair out of place.

"How . . ." is all the dumbfounded lawyer can get out, for a moment. He regains some composure and says, "I don't understand. You should be splattered all over Fifth Avenue, and yet you're here. How's that possible?"

"It's simple," says the reporter. "Right on this spot, the trans-Manhattan winds create a force so strong that they'll carry anyone who jumps around the building three times, and then deposit them right back where they started. Watch again." With that, he jumps again, and is tossed around the building three times before being deposited back on the platform. And again, with not so much as a hair out of place.

The lawyer is dumbfounded. "Let me try!" he says, and the reporter steps aside so that the lawyer can jump from where he had been standing.

The lawyer jumps and falls to his death.

Two men on the ground are looking at the body when they see the reporter emerge from the ground floor and head back to the convention. One man shakes his head and says, "That's the eighth one today. That Clark Kent sure hates lawyers."

 · L A W Y E R ·

 A lawyer, a man demonstrating the trans-Manhattan winds

 The Empire State Building

A superhero shows his evil side.

The Old Man at the Pearly Gates

St. Peter is just about to close the Pearly Gates one night when an old man shows up and asks for his help. "I'm looking for my son," the old man says. "He left when he was very young. I know that I am only a carpenter, but I beg you to help me find him. You'll know him by the holes in his hands and feet."

St. Peter immediately realizes that God is testing him, and that this must be Joseph, come to look for Jesus. "Please rest awhile while I get your son for you," he tells the carpenter.

Finding Jesus a few minutes later, St. Peter tells him that there is a carpenter waiting by the gate for the son that left  him as a young man. Jesus rushes to the old man.

"Father?" Jesus says.

The old man says, "Pinocchio?"

• P E A R L Y   G A T E S •

 An old man, St. Peter, Jesus

 Outside the Pearly Gates

Jesus and Pinocchio have a few things in common.

Trusty Silver Goes for Help

The Lone Ranger and Tonto are ambushed by a band of desperadoes. Trapped behind a large boulder, and outnumbered 10 to 2, their situation seems utterly hopeless. Knowing that they'll soon be out of ammunition, they both rack their brains for a solution to their predicament.

Suddenly, the Lone Ranger gets an idea. He lets out a whistle and Silver, his faithful steed, appears at his side. He whispers in Silver's ear, and sends the horse galloping off, past the band of desperadoes. "Tonto," the Lone Ranger says, "help is on the way."

"Tonto hope help come soon," the trusted sidekick says, "or else Tonto and Lone Ranger headed for big roundup in the sky."

They continue to trade gunfire with the desperadoes until they are almost out of bullets. The situation is beginning to look bleak when, at the last possible moment, Silver reappears with a beautiful naked woman on his back.

The Lone Ranger sees what Silver is carrying and screams, "Silver, you idiot! I said *posse!*"

• BAWDY •

The Lone Ranger, Tonto, desperadoes, Silver

The Old West

 Silver demonstrates his poor hearing.

How Tommy Drowned

Mrs. O'Hara is talking to Clancy the barkeep about the accidental death of her husband, Tommy. Clearly distraught at the unfortunate turn of events, she laments, "Oh, Clancy, it's just so hard to understand some things in this world. It seems so completely horrible that he fell into the vat of beer you keep in the back room and drowned."

"Ah," Clancy says, leaning back in his chair, giving thought to his words, "you have to console yourself with the knowledge that he had a full and happy life."

"Oh, I know," says the widow, "but it just seems like he suffered terribly. I mean, the coroner said that even though he fell in at midnight, he didn't actually drown until almost four in the mornin'. It just seems so strange. I can't get it out of me head. I wonder how you explain that . . ."

"Well, that's simple," says Clancy. "I saw him climb out two or three times to take a leak."

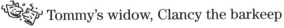

•BARROOM•

 Tommy's widow, Clancy the barkeep

 A bar

Clancy commiserates with the widow.

Imelda the Slut

A peasant farmer tells his wife that he's walking the ten miles to town. "Don't forget to pick up our bucket from the Johnsons!" she calls to him. He nods.

"And our anvil!" she adds. He nods again.

"And don't forget to buy two chickens!" He just keeps nodding.

"And one pig!"

"Enough!" he yells.

"One more thing," she says, as he heads out the door, "Watch out for that slut, Imelda."

"Of course, dear," he says. "Good-bye!"

With that, he heads out the door and into town. After buying the two chickens and the pig, he stops at the Johnson house and picks up his anvil and bucket. Arms loaded, he sets off for home.

Not twenty feet from town, he runs into Imelda. They walk together for a while, and once they are far enough from town that no one can see them, Imelda says, "I shouldn't walk with you. I know that you want to drag me into the fields and have your way with me."

"Don't be silly," the farmer says. "Besides, I am loaded up, as you can see. How would I be able to do that without losing my animals?"

"You are clever," she says. "You would put the pig down, and turn the bucket over and put it on top of the pig. You would put the anvil on the bucket so that the pig couldn't get away."

"Aha," he says. "And what would I do with the chickens?"

"Oh, I'll hold the chickens."

· BAWDY ·

A farmer, his wife, Imelda

The road from town

A slut lives up to her reputation.

119

Custer's Last Words

A famous painter is commissioned by a museum owner to portray one aspect of Custer's Last Stand. After months of research, he informs the owner that he will do an artistic rendering of Custer's last words, and he starts to work.

A year later, the painting is unveiled.

As the sheet is pulled away from the work, the crowd of art critics and art patrons gasps. There on the canvas are dozens of Native American couples, copulating in every position imaginable. In the center of them is a cow with a ring around its head.

The museum owner is shocked. "What is the meaning of this?!" he yells at the painter.

"I told you," says the painter, "that my painting would depict Custer's last words. Read the plaque."

And there, on the plaque at the bottom of the painting, are Custer's last words: "Holy Cow! Look at all those fucking Indians!"

· B A W D Y ·

 A painter, a museum owner

 A museum

 A literal interpretation of Custer's demise.

The Musical Bird
and Mouse

Joe, the drunk, comes into a bar and says to the bartender, "My good man, a tall glass of Johnnie Walker."

"Come on, Joe," says the bartender, "you know I can't serve you. You're already five hundred behind on your tab."

"Ah," says Joe, "wait till you see what I have to offer in exchange." Joe pulls a mouse, a parakeet, and a tiny white piano from his coat, and sets them on the bar. The mouse crawls over to the piano, and begins playing "Danny Boy," which the parakeet proceeds to sing.

"That's amazing!" says the bartender.

"What will you give me for them?" says Joe.

"I'll forgive your tab, and give you five thousand dollars for both animals."

"Done," says Joe. "Now, how about that Johnnie Walker?"

"Coming right up," the bartender says, and goes to get the drink. While he's doing that, the man on the next stool says to Joe, "You idiot! You could've got millions for animals like those! You got rooked, pal."

Joe laughs. "On the contrary; it's the bartender who was swindled. That bird can't sing—the mouse is a ventriloquist!"

· BARROOM ·

A bartender, Joe the drunk, a man sitting next to him

A bar

A drunk gets conned out of his prize animals.

The Profane Ceiling Painter

Roberto the great painter is finishing up his latest masterpiece, the ceiling of a wondrous cathedral, when Sister Mary comes in and calls to him from the bottom of the scaffolding, "Hey, Roberto!"

Startled, Roberto's hand slips and smudges the area he had just painted. "Son of a bitch!" he cries in anger. With that, the sky rolls with thunder, and the cathedral begins shaking violently. The scaffolding topples, and Roberto's flailing arms smudge his great work in a number of places. Roberto falls to the floor, but miraculously is not killed.

Frightened, he says to Sister Mary, "What have I done?"

"You have used profanity in the house of the Lord!" she says. "You must get down on your knees and beg for forgiveness!"

And Roberto does. "Dear God," he pleads, "forgive my weakness in your house. I am truly sorry." With that, the clouds part and the scaffolding miraculously rights itself. The smudges disappear from the painting, and Roberto finds himself lifted by some invisible force. In a moment he is on his back on the scaffolding, right where he was before he cursed.

Sister Mary, who can barely believe what she is seeing, says, "Son of a bitch!"

• R E L I G I O N •

 Roberto the painter, Sister Mary

A great cathedral

 A nun gives hypocritical advice.

The
Spelling Lesson

Miss Jones says to her third graders, "Today I'm going to have you each do three things: First, tell the class what your father's occupation is. Next, spell the name of his occupation. Then, explain what your father would do for us if he were here. Tommy?"

Tommy says, "My daddy's a cook. C-O-O-K. He would cook you all lunch."

"Very good," says Miss Jones. "Susie?"

Susie says, "My daddy's a broker. B-R-O-K-E-R. He would take your piggy banks and invest all your pennies for you."

"Very good," says Miss Jones. "Bobby?"

Bobby says, "My daddy's an electrician. E-L- uh, um, E-L-I, no, E-L- uh . . ."

"That's okay, Bobby," says Miss Jones. "You think about it, and we'll come back to you. Eddie?"

Little Eddie says, "My old man's a bookie. B-double O-K-I-E. He'd lay you five-to-one odds that this idiot will *never* figure out how to spell 'electrician.'"

• C L A S S R O O M •

 Miss Jones, Tommy, Susie, Bobby, Little Eddie

A classroom

Little Eddie teaches the class about bookies.

The Pig Farmer's Dilemma

 pig farmer is panicking. For some reason, his pigs don't seem to be reproducing. Knowing his livelihood is in jeopardy, he goes to the vet, and nervously explains the problem.

"Well . . ." the vet says, "there is one thing you can do, but it's really only a last resort."

"I'm desperate," the farmer says.

"You're not gonna like this," the vet tells him. "Why don't we wait a bit longer?"

"Look," the farmer says, "I don't have much time. If my pigs don't have piglets soon, I'll have to sell the farm and all of my earthly possessions. I'll do anything . . ."

The vet thinks for a moment, and says, "Okay, but I warned you: You're not going to like this. Here's what you do. Load all the female pigs into your truck in the morning, drive them into the deepest, darkest part of the woods, and . . . you have to have sex with every one of them."

"Oh my God," the farmer says, "I can't do that!"

"Well," the vet says, "you asked, and I'm telling you. That's what seems to work."

The farmer looks resigned. "How long will I have to do this?"

"Until they're pregnant," the vet shrugs.

"I know *that*," the farmer says. "I mean, how will I know when they're pregnant?"

"That's easy," the vet says. "Every morning when you wake up, look out the window. On the morning after a pig conceives, she rolls on her back in the mud. That's how you'll know."

The farmer thanks him and goes home. The next morning, he loads the pigs up in the truck, takes them to the deepest, darkest part of the woods, and has sex with each of them. The morning after, he rushes from his bed to the window and sees the pigs all wandering around . . . not one of them on her back, rolling around. He repeats the process, and still no luck. After doing this for a week, he grows so desperate that he loads the pigs up really early in the morning, takes them to the deepest, darkest part of the woods, and has sex with each of them *twice*. Exhausted and becoming resigned to the fact that his pigs will never conceive, he falls into bed.

The next morning, he oversleeps a bit. When he wakes up, he yells to his wife, "Please, honey, look out the window and tell me what the pigs are doing. I haven't the strength to look for myself."

His wife goes to the window, and says, "Oh my God . . . this is incredible!"

"What is it?" he asks, hopefully.

"The pigs," she says, "have loaded *themselves* into the truck, and one of them's honking the horn!"

· **B A W D Y** ·

A pig farmer, a vet, the pig farmer's wife

A pig farm

Repeated sex with a corral of pigs

How Jesus Golfs

God, Jesus, and Moses are enjoying an incognito game of golf. On the first tee, God hits a beautiful 3-wood, Moses does the same, and Jesus pulls out a 5-iron. "This is the way Jack Nicklaus would play the shot," he tells the other two. His shot passes God's and Moses' by a few yards.

On their second shots, God and Moses each hit a nice 7-iron shot, leaving the ball just short of the green. Jesus pulls out his 5-iron and tells the other two, "This is what Jack Nicklaus would do," before putting the ball past God's and Moses', right on the edge of the green.

God and Moses, each with a pitching wedge, land their balls on the green and very close to the hole. Jesus shakes his head. "You know what Nicklaus would do?" he asks them. "He'd use the sand wedge from the short rough to get a little more height on the shot." With that, he hits the ball with the sand wedge, putting it over the green and into a pond. Disgusted with himself, he walks out onto the pond to retrieve his ball.

A golfer who had been playing behind the Holy Threesome walks over to Moses, and not recognizing him, asks, "Who does that guy think he is, Jesus Christ?"

Moses says, "He *is* Jesus Christ, but he *thinks* he's Jack Nicklaus."

• R E L I G I O N / G O L F •

God, Jesus, Moses, a golfer

A golf course

Jesus tries to be like Jack Nicklaus.

Why Mommy
Can't Answer the Door

traveling salesman rings the doorbell of a small house and a little boy comes to the door. "Hello, little boy," says the salesman. "Is your mommy at home?"

"She's busy," says the boy. "She's in the backyard having sex with a goat."

"She's what?" says the salesman.

"She's out back having sex with a goat," the boy says.

"Little boy, are you lying to me?"

"No, sir," says the little boy. "My mommy's always in the backyard having sex with a goat."

"And doesn't that bother you?" asks the salesman.

"Na-ah-ah-ah-ah," says the boy.

• B A W D Y •

 A traveling salesman, a little goat-boy

 The front porch

A little goat-boy answers the door.

The Lawyer Who Died Unexpectedly

Upon death, a lawyer finds himself in a line at the Pearly Gates, waiting to speak to St. Peter. When it's his turn, he finds St. Peter at a desk in front of a computer terminal. He is very distraught and anxious to plead his case.

"There must be some mistake," says the lawyer. "I can't possibly be dead. I was sitting at my desk working on a very important case that might make me a partner, and the next thing I know I'm here. Nothing fell on me, I didn't have a heart attack, I wasn't sick . . . what am I doing here?"

St. Peter asks him his name, punches it into the computer, and waits patiently for it to register. "Ah," he tells the lawyer, "it says that you died of old age."

"Old age?" the lawyer says. "How could I die of old age when I'm 34?"

St. Peter shakes his head while looking long and hard at the screen and says, "That's odd; according to your billing hours, you're 106."

• *L A W Y E R / P E A R L Y   G A T E S* •

 A lawyer, St. Peter

The Pearly Gates

 A lawyer is baffled by his own death.

The Church's Mysterious Peeling Paint

A man is hired by his parish priest to paint the new church. On the first day of work, he notices that he can save paint by thinning it with water. By the time he has finished, he has secretly saved enough paint to go home and paint his own house.

One year later, he notices that the paint on his house is peeling. Realizing that this must mean the paint on the church is in a similar state, he is racked with guilt at his actions and goes to the parish priest to confess his sin.

"Father," he says, "I have done a terrible thing. Though I meant no harm, I thinned the paint that you gave me for the church so that I could use the extra to paint my own home. I didn't realize that the water would make the paint start to peel so quickly. I feel horrible about it and I'm fully prepared to make reparations. What can I do to make it up to you and to the parish?"

The priest thinks for a moment, and says, "Repaint, and thin no more."

• G R O A N E R •

 A painter, a priest

A new church

 A painter cheats the church on its paint.

The Talking Farm Animals

A traveling salesman asks a local farmer if he can spend the night, as his car has broken down nearby and will take a day to fix.

"Sure," says the farmer. "If you don't mind sleeping in the barn with the animals."

"Not at all," says the salesman. "Thank you."

The next morning, the salesman is knocking frantically on the front door. When the farmer answers, he explains, "You won't believe this, but your animals can talk."

The farmer laughs, "You must have been drunk, sir."

The salesman says, "No, I was quite sober. I talked to them all night, and I can prove it."

"Okay," says the farmer, "prove it."

"Well, your cow Bessie told me that she nearly died giving birth to the calf, and how you stayed with her all night, taking care of her."

The farmer stares wide-eyed, as the salesman continues. "And your pig Hilda told me about the time she knocked the gas lamp over and almost burned down the barn."

The farmer is amazed. "Why, you couldn't know those things unless the animals *did* talk to you, because I've never told anyone else about either of them . . ." His voice trails off for a moment, as if something is occurring to him. "Say," he says, "my sheep Lulu didn't tell you anything, did she? 'Cause she's known to be a liar."

· B A W D Y ·

 A farmer, a traveling salesman

 A farmhouse

 Talking animals expose a farmer.

The Gas Jockey and the Old Couple

An old man and his wife are driving through upstate New York when they stop in a gas station to fill up. The attendant, trying to make conversation, says to the old man, "I see from your license plate that you're from Vermont."

The wife, who is hard of hearing, says, "WHAT'D HE SAY?"

The old man yells in her ear, "HE SAYS HE SEES WE'RE FROM VERMONT."

"Oh," she says.

The attendant says to the old man, "That's a beautiful state."

The wife asks, "WHAT'D HE SAY?"

The old man yells in her ear, "HE SAYS VERMONT IS A BEAUTIFUL STATE."

"Oh," she says.

The attendant leans in and whispers to the old man, "I had the worst sex of my life in Vermont."

The wife asks, "WHAT'D HE SAY?"

The old man says to her, "HE SAID HE THINKS HE KNOWS YOU."

· GENERAL / BAWDY ·

An old couple, a young gas jockey

A rural gas station

An old man loses patience with his deaf wife.

The Foul-Mouthed Parrot and the Freezer

Two parrots are sitting in their cage when their new owner comes downstairs one morning. "Hello," he cheerfully says to them.

"Hello," squawks the first parrot.

"Go to hell," squawks the second parrot.

"What did you say?" says the owner. "Do that again and I'll fix you."

The next morning, the owner comes downstairs and again, cheerfully says, "Hello."

"Hello," squawks the first parrot.

"Eat shit," squawks the second parrot.

"What did you say?" says the owner. "I mean it. One more time and you're going in the freezer."

When the owner goes out, the first parrot decides he should warn the second parrot. "You'd better shape up or he's gonna put you in the freezer."

"Oh, please," says the second parrot. "He's only bluffing. He'll only put me in for five minutes, just to scare me. You wait and see. He won't follow through."

The next morning, the owner comes downstairs and says, "Hello."

"Hello," squawks the first parrot.

"Screw you," squawks the second parrot.

"That's it," says the enraged owner. "Into the freezer with you." He puts the second parrot in the freezer and slams the door. Five minutes later, he takes the parrot out of the freezer and puts him back in the cage.

"Now," he says. "Hello."

"Hello," squawks the first parrot.

"Hello," squawks the second parrot.

Happy, the owner walks away. As soon as he does, the first parrot says, "Why did you back down? You were right all along. He only put you in the freezer for five minutes."

"Maybe so," says the second parrot, "but I'm not pushing him."

"Why not?" asks the first parrot.

"Because there's a chicken in that freezer who must have done something that *really* pissed him off."

· **B A W D Y** ·

 Two parrots, their owner

The owner's house

A parrot learns some manners.